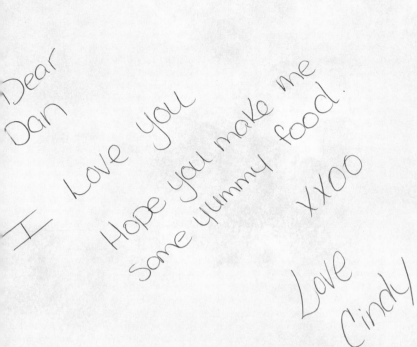

Dear
Dan
I Love you
Hope you make me
Some yummy food.
XXOO

Love
Cindy

THE APPETIZER BIBLE

Publications International, Ltd.

Favorite Brand Name Recipes at www.fbnr.com

Contributing writer: Marilyn Pocius

Pictured on the front cover *(counterclockwise from top left):* Apricot-Chicken Pot Stickers *(page 262),* Dreamy Orange Cheesecake Dip *(page 156),* Tuna in Crispy Won Ton Cup *(page 182),* Savory Chicken Satay *(page 220)* and Triangle Tostada *(page 104).*
Pictured on the back cover *(clockwise from top):* Pizza Fondue *(page 120),* Can't Get Enough Chicken Wings *(page 214),* Hidden Valley® Torta *(page 152)* and Chicken Roll *(page 192).*

ISBN-13: 978-1-4127-2345-9
ISBN-10: 1-4127-2345-0

Library of Congress Control Number: 2006900099

Manufactured in China.

8 7 6 5 4 3 2 1

Microwave Cooking: Microwave ovens vary in wattage. Use the cooking times as guidelines and check for doneness before adding more time.

Preparation/Cooking Times: Preparation times are based on the approximate amount of time required to assemble the recipe before cooking, baking, chilling or serving. These times include preparation steps such as measuring, chopping and mixing. The fact that some preparations and cooking can be done simultaneously is taken into account. Preparation of optional ingredients and serving suggestions is not included.

Contents

A TASTE FOR APPETIZERS

Why do appetizers seem to be everyone's favorite course? It could be the variety—appetizers offer many flavorful bites of lots of different dishes. Or it might be that eating them with your hands is encouraged. Maybe it's because appetizers let even picky eaters try something new without making a major commitment. Most likely it's because food always tastes better when it's served with conversation and friends.

Whether it's oysters on the half shell or tried-and-true onion dip and potato chips, appetizers set the mood for any get-together. How could a picnic begin without deviled eggs? Who would want to go to a Super Bowl party that didn't have guacamole and chips? And a glass of red wine simply doesn't taste as delicious without some cheese and crackers.

For the home cook, appetizers can be a creative way to please a crowd without overspending or overworking. Most hors d'oeuvres are relatively easy to prepare. Many can be made in advance. They can be served in a

multitude of ways, from just setting them out on a table ahead of time to hiring a waiter (or cajoling your kids) to pass trays filled with goodies. Variety is the name of the game, so if one offering is less than perfect, nobody even notices. (Try that with a Thanksgiving turkey!) With proper planning, appetizers also let you, the cook, join the party instead of being stuck in the kitchen.

The Appetizer Bible will help you plan nibbles, noshes, canapés and hors d'ouevres for every sort of get-together whether you're an accomplished hostess or just throwing your first party. There's information on how much to serve, how to serve it and how to do it all easily. Whether you need to know how to handle phyllo dough or make a pork terrine, or you just want a simple recipe for guacamole, you'll find it here.

More than 150 recipes will tempt you with so many ideas, it won't be long before you're looking for an excuse to invite friends over.

A Quick Course in First Courses

Appetizers are called by many different names: first courses, hors d'oeuvres, canapés, finger foods, starters. While there are some distinct definitions, it's more important to remember that whatever you call them, appetizers are a prelude to the meal. They are meant to delight and awaken taste buds, not to fill people up.

What is usually referred to as a first course is most often served at the table as a part of a meal. In a restaurant this could be a salad, a shrimp cocktail or just a small portion of a flavorful pasta dish. Of course, hosting a dinner party with multiple courses is hardly a regular occurrence in most homes. Entertaining today is much less formal and lots more fun. Classic first courses, such as stuffed mushrooms or deviled eggs, are still favorites, but it's easier and more conversation-friendly to serve them with drinks in the living room or on the deck where guests can mix and mingle.

Hors d'oeuvre is simply the French word for appetizer that sounds a bit snooty (maybe because it's so hard to spell and pronounce!). Hors d'oeuvres can be simple raw vegetables served with a dip or fancy puff pastries filled with exotic ingredients. Canapés are small open face sandwiches, either hot or cold, on toasted bread, crackers or pastry. For more definitions, see the glossary (pages 45–48).

Appetizers are enjoying a well-deserved popularity these days. American cooking allows us to sample from a vast array of cuisines and ethnic specialties. Because a small bite of something flavorful is an excellent opportunity to try a new taste without risk, delicious dishes like Mexican guacamole and Italian bruschetta have quickly become popular American-style hors d'oeuvres. Pity the poor French who count escargot (snails) as their most celebrated first course! Snails can be delicious, of course; see the recipe for Patrician Escargots (page 52).

What Makes an Appetizer an Appetizer?

Almost any dish can be turned into an appetizer—just cut the portion size down to a few bites. It's really when and how the food is served that counts. While there are no hard and fast rules, there are guidelines for what makes the best appetizers.

1. Since each guest will only have a bite of two of each hors d'oeuvre, flavors should come through loud and clear.

2. Think small. Whether hot or cold, the size of an appetizer should be limited to a few bites.

3. Unless appetizers will be served at a table with silverware, make them easy to eat. Hand-held treats allow guests to hold a drink in one hand, keep a conversation going and still enjoy the food.

4. It's best to avoid foods that are messy or drippy. Try to keep juicy ingredients contained in pastry cups or wrapped up for easy handling. Even dips shouldn't be so runny they're likely to stain party clothes.

5. Presentation is important. Color, texture and even the arrangement of appetizers make a huge difference in how your guests will experience them. Everyone tastes first with their eyes.

6. Hors d'oeuvres should never seem heavy, dull or filling. Rich flavorful foods, on the other hand, such as pâté or olives, work well because small bites of them can tantalize taste buds.

Appetizers by the Numbers

How Many?

How many appetizers will you need? The answer is, "it depends." Many factors need to be considered. For instance, if your get-together is planned as a prelude to a full dinner, you need fewer appetizers. Who your guests are matters, too. Hungry guys will demolish a platter full of shrimp in a heartbeat. Appetites will be greater in the late afternoon or early evening than post dinnertime. As always, it's better to have too much food than not enough. The chart on the next page gives basic rules of thumb for calculating the number of small bites you'll need for an average two hour get-together with dinner afterwards.

A First Course in French

Hors d'oeuvre literally means "outside of the work." The "work" is the main meal and hors d'oeuvres are savory finger foods generally served with cocktails (aperitifs). In French, an entrée is actually the first course at a sit-down, formal meal. Think of it as an "entry" to the meal. In English, of course, an entrée IS the main course. All of this doesn't matter one bit, unless you're in France ordering dinner!

Number of Guests	Number of Appetizers	Varieties of Appetizer
8 to 10	40 to 70	3 different types
12 to 16	60 to 96	4 different types
18 to 30	90 to 180	5 different types (1 or more hot)
32 to 46	160 to 276	7 different types (2 or more hot)

These amounts assume individual pieces, so if you are also serving dips, nuts or cheeses, adjust numbers downward.

Adjust the numbers according to your particular circumstances. If dinner will be several hours away, or everyone has just come in from a game of tennis, you'll need more food. On the other hand, a ladies' book club can usually make do with fewer hors d'oeuvres.

Original Ranch® Spinach Dip (page 142)

What Kind?

Again, the answer depends on the situation and the guests. Variety is important. While each person may consume five appetizers, they probably aren't going to eat five of one kind. Consider dietary preferences, too. It's wise to include at least one vegetarian offering and to have something light for folks who watch calorie or fat intake.

The type of appetizers should also be varied. Five dips wouldn't make a very nice display, nor would five appetizers in pastry cups. Choose some canapé or sandwich-type appetizers, something wrapped or rolled, simple fruits or vegetables cut into bite-size pieces, shrimp or a heartier meat-based hors d'oeuvre. There is no correct formula. Just mix it up and provide contrasting flavors and textures.

While you're in the planning stage, imagine the actual event. Will you be serving from a buffet table? Can you set up "stations," that is, small tables located throughout the room that each hold an array of nibbles? Should appetizers all be hand-held or will forks be needed? What about plates? It's usually not a good idea to serve something that needs to be cut with a knife unless there is plenty of seating. Even then, it's hard to balance a drink, a napkin, a plate and cutlery on your lap.

Hot appetizers are lovely, but they do require last minute attention. Plan your party so that cold dips or crudités are being served while the hot items are in the oven. Don't try to do too much, especially at the last minute.

Need Help?

The best parties are the ones the host or hostess enjoys. Keep things simple. It's perfectly fine to serve some store-bought appetizers along with home-made. You probably don't need or want a caterer to handle a casual get-together, but that doesn't mean you won't enjoy yourself more if you have some assistance at party time. Enlist neighborhood teens to help with serving and cleanup. A local caterer can also recommend servers you can hire on an hourly basis for less than you'd think. Being able to spend more time with your guests is invaluable.

And seeing that everything is under control frees your guests to enjoy the festivities without feeling obligated to help out.

When Appetizers Are Dinner

The exception to the rule that appetizers should stimulate the palate and not fill guests up is a get-together where appetizers make the meal. Cocktail parties often fall into this category, especially when they are scheduled in the early evening. It's too early for guests to have had dinner, but it's late enough that everyone is hungry. An all-appetizer party is also a good choice for the hostess who wants to entertain without the limitations of a standard dinner party. There's no need to have a huge dining room or service for 12. Many people also prefer an appetizer party because it's less formal and lets guests mix and mingle as they like.

The same general guidelines apply for keeping finger food easy to handle and eat. If appetizers are going to be dinner, however, it's a good idea to include some heartier items, such as shrimp, meatballs, chicken wings and the like. Variety is more important than ever. Try to mix things up with vegetable nibbles, fresh fruit pieces and a cheese tray. You will probably want to offer some sweet bites, too.

Five Nibble No-No's

1. No greasy or sloppy food that will stain at first bite

2. No exploding food, such as whole cherry tomatoes or overstuffed dumplings

3. No overloaded skewers or toothpicks; always provide a place to discard used ones

4. No super hot food that will burn mouth. (Extremely spicy is not a good idea either)

5. No extra-heavy doses of garlic and onion—conversation is important

Quantities may need to be adjusted upwards. The usual number quoted by caterers is 7 to 8 appetizers per person instead of the 5 or 6 per person recommended for a party that precedes dinner. As always, consider who your guests are and err on the side of too much food.

If you're planning an all-appetizer party, it's crucial to figure out serving options and get help if you need it. It's also an opportunity to ask guests to bring their favorite appetizers and add to the fun and the variety of food being presented.

The Portable Appetizer

When you're asked to bring an appetizer to a party, remember that there will be limited kitchen space and not much refrigerator room or oven time available either. The host or hostess may also be too busy to help you get your hors d'oeuvres on the table.

The best appetizers for travel are those that require nothing more than transferring to a platter or bowl. If you have a special serving dish, bring it along. Dips, cold shrimp and crudités fall into this category. To keep cold things cold, place them in a cooler with ice packs for the journey if it will take more than a few minutes.

Hors d'oeuvres that will be served hot should be fully cooked in advance so they only require rewarming. If you will need a baking sheet other than a standard sort, bring it along, or at least check with your host or hostess to see what he or she has available.

Items that need complicated assembly that can't be done ahead of time, for instance, elaborately stacked canapés, should be saved for another occasion.

Maple-Glazed Meatballs (page 216)

From Bottom to Top

The simplest appetizers are what amount to open-face sandwiches. These are usually called canapés, but bruschetta and crostini also fall into this category. The base for these nibbles is nothing more than toasted bread. But what kind of bread? The possibilities are endless. There is even a traditional type of white bread baked in a special square pan with a cover to give it a fine, dense texture perfect for cutting into canapés. It is called a pullman loaf or "pain de mie" in French. A good quality, thinly sliced sandwich bread from the supermarket will serve the same purpose. Look for a loaf with a firm texture. Soft, limp bread won't hold up under a topping.

Choose bread that will complement whatever topping you have in mind, and don't limit yourself to white bread. Think about varying the shape of your bread pieces or toasts, too. This is easily done with a small cookie cutter (about 1½ inches in diameter is perfect). If you aren't toasting the bread, keep the pieces covered with plastic wrap or a damp towel so they won't dry out while you're working. For perfectly tailored canapés, spread the slices with flavored butter and

other toppings before cutting them into shapes so the spread covers right up to the edges.

It's easy to create toast cups (also called croustades) to hold moist fillings securely. Use a standard or mini muffin pan as your mold. Cut squares or rounds of thinly sliced bread, brush them with melted butter or olive oil and press each piece firmly into a muffin cup. Then bake in a preheated 375°F oven until the edges are browned. The same technique will work with flour tortillas or soft corn tortillas.

The Toast of the Party

You don't need a recipe for making toast, but here are some tips on toasting bread to be used as a base for hors d'oeuvres.

1. Slightly stale bread toasts better than fresh.

2. The toast (and the canapé) will only be as good as the quality of the bread.

3. Toast bread under a preheated broiler. Watch carefully and turn the bread frequently until it is evenly browned.

4. Each variety of bread and individual slice will toast in a different amount of time depending on moistness and thickness. Toast the same kind of pieces on one baking sheet and be prepared to turn the sheet if the bread is browning unevenly.

5. Grilling bread instead of toasting can be a nice touch and adds a whisper of smoke that works well with full-flavored hors d'oeuvres, such as pâté or olive spread.

Can You Top That?

Toppings for toasts can be straightforward (cream cheese and salami) or incredibly complex. The best are simply good combinations of flavors, many of them familiar. (Even peanut butter and jelly has sometimes found its way to the hors d'oeuvres tray!) Generally a canapé starts with a spread, which helps keep the bread from getting soggy, followed by a topping and perhaps a garnish. The chart below has some mix and match suggestions. When choosing ingredients, pair one that is somewhat bland with a stronger flavor. For a specific example, see the recipe for Crab Canapés (page 76).

Canapé Ingredients

Spreads	Toppings	Garnish
cream cheese	deli meats	pickle slice
deviled ham	cheese	capers
flavored butter	seafood bits	lemon peel
sun-dried tomato pesto	sliced olives	basil leaf
hummus	mushrooms	red pepper bits
chive cream cheese	smoked salmon	dill sprig
garlic-herb cheese spread	chopped egg	parsley
nut butters	fruit slices or spreads	chopped nuts

"Tea" Sandwiches

The traditional cucumber sandwich served at a British high tea is fine in its place, but many other sandwiches make excellent appetizers. Just think of your favorite combinations and reimagine them in small portions. Those popular 10-foot-long party sub sandwiches are an example of this principle.

One of the tricks to sandwich-style hors d'oeuvres is constructing them so that they hold up well and will not fall apart when cut into smaller sizes. You'll also need to find ingredients that won't soak into the bread or leak out. Tomatoes may be great in a sandwich you're eating immediately, but not in one that will stay out on a buffet table for an hour or two. Bread should be sturdy, not flimsy. Buttering the slices offers some protection from wet ingredients as well.

Since these bites will be small, substitute more flavorful fixings for old standbys. Think prosciutto or smoked salmon instead of deli ham, goat cheese instead of American, smoked turkey instead of chicken, focaccia bread instead of white.

Spreads needn't be limited to butter, either. Pesto (basil or sun-dried tomato), tapenade and flavored cream cheese all work well.

Making Flavored Butter or Cream Cheese

It is easy to do and adds an extra touch of flavor and elegance to hors d'oeuvres. Just add 2 to 3 tablespoons of finely chopped herbs to one stick (½ cup) of softened butter or a small (3-ounce) package of cream cheese. Mix by hand or with a mixer until blended. You can use one herb or a combination. Basil, chives, parsley, oregano, mint and tarragon are all good choices. Grated lemon or lime peel, garlic or shallots can also be added in the same fashion.

Beyond Bread

Many forms of pastry are used in making appetizers. The two that you'll most often find in recipes are puff pastry dough and phyllo dough. Both types can be purchased in the freezer case of any supermarket. (Making either puff pastry or phyllo from scratch requires skill [and time!] that most home cooks don't have. Besides, the frozen products are usually of excellent quality.) Check individual recipes, but many appetizers made with pastry can be prepared ahead of time, frozen and reheated when needed.

Handling Puff Pastry

Puff pastry is made of countless layers of thin, crisp pastry each separated by a film of butter. When it is baked, the steam created by the moisture in the butter causes the layers to puff.

To thaw puff pastry, separate the sheets and take out as many as you'll need. Wrap and return any unused portion to the freezer. You'll need to thaw the pastry in the refrigerator for about four hours (a whole package takes six). If you're in a hurry, you can separate the sheets, cover each one with plastic wrap and thaw at cool room temperature. They will be ready to work with in about 30 minutes. The refrigerator method is preferred, however, since the pastry thaws more evenly.

Chicken & Rice Puffs (page 184)

Work with one pastry sheet at a time and keep the rest refrigerated. Keeping puff pasty cool is important so that the butter doesn't melt before it gets to the oven. If the pastry seems to be getting warm and soft, return it the refrigerator for a while. For extra-thin layers, puff pastry may be rolled to ¼-inch thickness before shaping. To cut shapes, use a sharp knife or cookie cutter. To seal filled pastries, brush the edges with a mixture of beaten egg and water (1 egg with 2 or 3 tablespoons of water). Then pinch or press the edges together.

Make sure to preheat the oven to the temperature in the recipe. If you forget, return the pastry to the refrigerator while you wait. Maximum "puff" requires the butter to be cold when it enters the hot oven. If you use a dark colored baking sheet, you may need a shorter baking time than indicated. (Never bake puff pastry in a microwave or toaster oven.)

For recipes using puff pastry, see Chicken & Rice Puffs (page 184) and Pepper Cheese Cocktail Puffs (page 278).

Handling Phyllo Dough

Phyllo dough is very similar to puff pasty. The important difference is that with phyllo you brush each layer of pastry with butter yourself, instead of purchasing a dough where the layers are already prepared.

Phyllo is Greek for "leaf." Each sheet of dough has been stretched as paper thin as a leaf, so you can practically see through it. A one-pound box of frozen phyllo contains about twenty 17×12-inch sheets rolled up. Working with phyllo is a bit trickier than puff pastry, but once you understand the basics, it's not at all difficult.

The dough must be thawed in the refrigerator. If you attempt to thaw it at room temperature, too much moisture may enter the package and the layers will stick together. Remove the package from the freezer to the refrigerator at least 24 hours before you want to use it. Don't even open it up; just place it directly in the refrigerator. Thaw the entire package even if you don't need it all, since separating frozen sheets is next to impossible. Unused phyllo will last in the refrigerator for up to two weeks and can also be refrozen.

Prepare any fillings and allow them to cool before you take the phyllo out. Assemble the other things you'll need, depending on the recipe. Unwrap and unfold the phyllo carefully to avoid cracks. Place it on a clean, flat surface and cover it immediately with plastic wrap. Place a clean, damp dish towel over the plastic wrap to keep the dough soft and pliable. Since the sheets are so incredibly thin, phyllo dries out almost instantly. Once it dries, the dough becomes brittle and impossible to work with.

Take out one sheet at a time to brush with butter or oil. Use a soft pastry brush and work quickly from the edges towards the center. You can also use a spray bottle of vegetable oil or nonstick cooking spray. Work quickly and if the phyllo tears, don't fret, just patch it with another piece. After all, the only layer that will be visible is the one on top!

For recipes using phyllo dough, see Spinach Feta Triangles (page 80), Rice & Artichoke Phyllo Triangles (page 204) and Ham and Cheese Strudels with Mustard Sauce (page 202).

Both puff pastry and phyllo are amazingly versatile. They can be folded around fillings in many different shapes, prebaked into cups or cones, or used to line tart pans. You can often purchase preformed cups or shells in your grocer's freezer to make your life even easier.

Rice & Artichoke
Phyllo Triangles (page 204)

Getting Wrapped Up

Enclosing a filling in a wrapper makes finger food easy to hold and eat. From pigs in a blanket to Vietnamese summer rolls, wraps and rolls make great hors d'oeuvres. There are dozens of premade wrappers to choose from. Asian egg roll or wonton wrappers work well for many appetizers whether they are Asian-inspired or all-American. Refrigerated biscuit dough and crescent rolls are perfect for creating a quick stuffed pastry or rolling around sausage or

asparagus. Ordinary sandwich bread can be rolled thinly and used as a wrap, too. And don't forget phyllo and puff pastry dough (covered in the previous pages).

Asian Wrappers

Available fresh or frozen in most supermarkets, wonton wrappers are easy to use and serve a multitude of functions. The variety of shapes and sizes, as well as all the different names for these items can seem confusing at first, but virtually all Asian wrappers are interchangeable.

Wonton wrappers are also called egg roll, dumpling or pot sticker wrappers or skins. These thin sheets are usually available in packages of 20 to 30 in either squares or circles and can be found in the refrigerated produce section or supermarket freezer case. Fresh wrappers are available in Asian markets. Gyoza skins are the Japanese version of the same sort of wrap.

All of these paper-thin pastries are made from a flour, egg and water dough. After being wrapped around a filling, they may be steamed, fried, baked or boiled. Spring roll wrappers are virtually identical but are usually made only from flour and water and are generally a bit thinner than wonton wrappers.

Thaw frozen Asian wrappers in the refrigerator right in the package. They will keep for about a week in the refrigerator and most may be refrozen. To enclose a filling, you can roll, fold and pinch or pleat the wrapper into a packet, or gather the top like a purse. To help the packets stay sealed, brush a little water on the edge of the wrapper with your finger first. See recipes for Apricot-Chicken Pot Stickers (page 262) and Steamed Pork & Shrimp Dumplings (page 260).

Rice paper wrappers are a bit harder to find, but are worth seeking out in Asian markets. Look for dried, almost clear round sheets stacked in plastic boxes in the grocery aisle, not the refrigerator or freezer. After a brief soak in warm water, rice paper becomes stretchy and translucent. It makes a striking-looking wrap because you can see the colorful contents through the wrapper. See the recipe for Vietnamese Summer Rolls (page 268) for an example.

Tortillas and Flat Breads

Tortillas are the Latin American version of flat bread and perfect for making many kinds of wraps. Flour tortillas are easy to find in flavorful (and colorful) versions, including tomato, cilantro and garlic. Flour tortillas are flexible enough to spread with a filling and then roll up jelly-roll fashion. Cut into slices, this creates a lovely pinwheel appetizer that looks fancy with minimum work. For the prettiest results choose colorful ingredients that are

Quesadillas with olives and Jack cheese

fairly dry so they won't make the wrapper soggy or greasy.

Corn or flour tortillas can also be used for quesadillas, which are rather like grilled cheese sandwiches from south of the border. Don't limit them to Mexican flavors since quesadillas work with almost any combination of ingredients that includes a cheese or spread to act as a "glue" to hold the two sides together. See the sidebar for suggestions.

Quesadilla Combos

mozzarella, basil and tomato

thinly sliced ham and Cheddar

shredded chicken and prepared pesto

roast beef, cream cheese and horseradish

olives, Jack cheese and cilantro

crab meat and Swiss cheese

prosciutto and Brie cheese

mushrooms and goat cheese

pear or apple slices and Gorgonzola cheese

crumbled bacon, guacamole and pepper jack cheese

grilled chicken and roasted red pepper purée

The pocket in pita bread makes it easy to stuff with many kinds of fillings. Mini pitas are great for appetizer-sized sandwiches. Lavash (also called mountain or cracker bread), a Mediterranean flat bread, is a round or rectangle of thin dough, perfect for rolling or stuffing.

Turning Over a New Leaf

Using lettuce leaves for wrappers adds a fresh taste and a bit of crunch to appetizers. Experiment with red or green leaf, Bibb, romaine or iceberg lettuce. Each has its advantages. Bibb or leaf lettuce is the perfect size for rolling around a single serving of filling. Romaine lettuce stands up to stronger flavors and iceberg adds a pleasing crunch. Red or green cabbage leaves should be blanched before filling. Napa cabbage, large spinach leaves and even large mint leaves can also become wraps.

Radicchio, the slightly bitter Italian salad green, comes in small, tight heads that are a distinctive reddish-purple color. Its unique flavor complements a variety of fillings. Wrap radicchio around goat cheese and tomatoes, then grill the packets. Or use the natural cup shape of radicchio leaves as a container for a creamy dip.

Dipping Sauces

Many wraps and rolls are traditionally served with a dipping sauce. For Asian dishes this is usually a soy sauce-based dip. Quesadillas can be accompanied by salsas of all kinds. Many prepared dipping sauces, such as dumpling sauce and Asian peanut sauce, are readily available in the supermarket. Check the ethnic aisles and also the sauce and salad dressing section. Bottled marinades and salad dressings can often be used as is, or with a few modifications, for a dipping sauce. To make a store-bought dipping sauce look and taste a little more homemade, add a sprinkling of green onion, fresh herbs or brightly colored chili pepper slivers to the bowl.

Chicken Wraps (page 196)

Crêpes Aren't Just for Dessert

Versatile, easy-to-make crêpes are elegant wrappers for appetizers. (A basic recipe is on page 293.) If you can make pancakes, you can make crêpes. The procedure is almost identical. You don't need a special crêpe pan, either. Any small nonstick skillet with sloping sides will do. Crêpes can be wrapped or folded around fillings of all kinds. Think of them as the French version of tortillas.

Crêpes are excellent party food since they can be prepared in advance and freeze beautifully. Cool crêpes on a rack, then stack them and wrap them airtight or slip them into a resealable food storage bag. (Don't worry, they won't stick together.) Crêpes will keep for a day or two in the refrigerator and a month in the freezer. Thaw in the refrigerator or, if you're in a hurry, wrap the crêpes in foil and place them in a 250°F oven for 30 minutes until warmed. Of course, if you're really pressed for time, you can purchase ready-made crêpes at most supermarkets.

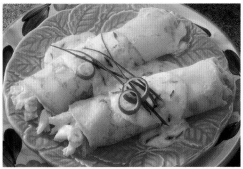

Seafood Crêpes (page 292)

Experience Crêpe Success

1. Use a whisk to make the batter if mixing by hand. Add some of the flour to the eggs, whisking out lumps as you go. Then alternate adding milk and flour. If the batter seems lumpy, strain it through a fine sieve. (Mixing the batter in a food processor or blender minimizes lumps.)

2. The batter should be the consistency of heavy cream. If it's too thick and difficult to pour, whisk in a little water.

3. Let the batter rest before cooking the crêpes. Resting lets the flour thoroughly absorb the liquid and you'll get better results.

4. You may need to adjust the heat level as you cook since the pan will heat up and cool down with each crêpe you make.

5. Wait until the edges of a cooked crêpe lift a little from the pan before attempting to turn it. You can use a spatula, or carefully pick up the edge with your fingers to turn the crêpe.

6. Don't panic if a few crêpes fall apart or come out misshapen. Even experienced crêpe makers mess up the first few. Ugly crêpes taste just as good, so relax and eat the evidence!

Dips, Dunks & Spreads

Quick Dip

Combine 8 ounces softened cream cheese and ⅓ cup prepared pesto. Serve with vegetables, chips or crackers.

Dips and spreads are favorites with guests and cooks alike. They're easy to put together, delicious to eat and fun to serve. Classic onion dip still has a place of honor on the buffet table. (See page 54 for a recipe for The Famous Lipton® California Dip.) More recent favorites include ethnic specialties, such as hummus and Asian peanut dip. These exciting new flavors don't require exotic ingredients and are welcome additions to any cook's repertoire.

The difference between a spread and a dip is nothing more than the thickness of the mixture. To turn a spread into a dip, thin it with cream, lemon juice, vinegar or mayonnaise. Most dip recipes are very forgiving and are a great place to exercise your creativity. For a dip based on sour cream, cream cheese or mayonnaise, try substituting yogurt, crème fraîche or a soft cheese. Instead of tomatoes, create a salsa from peaches, pineapple or other fresh fruit.

Seasonings can be adjusted to suit your taste. Do you hate cilantro? Replace it with flat leaf parsley or fresh oregano. Watching your calories or fat? Low-fat or fat-free sour cream can often be substituted for the full-fat variety. In a flavorful dip, you'll hardly notice. You can add a special touch to a store-bought dip by stirring in chopped fresh herbs at the last minute. A squeeze of lemon or lime juice will also perk up a salsa or other dip.

Slow cooker used to serve a cheese dip

When adjusting seasonings remember that certain flavors need time to develop, so if you prepare it in advance, taste the dip again right before serving. Hot pepper seasonings, such as ground red pepper and jalapeño, become stronger over time. Flavors are somewhat muted by cold, so they need to be stronger if a dip will be served chilled.

Bowl Them Over

How a dip is served can make a big difference in how it tastes. Think about the ideal temperature for your dip. Does it need to be warm, hot, cold or room temperature? To keep hot dips hot, you can use a small slow cooker or fondue pot. If you need a dip or spread to stay cold, place the serving bowl in another larger bowl filled with crushed ice.

You can purchase specially designed chip and dip bowls, but they're certainly not necessary. Think beyond the bowl and consider serving a dip or spread in an edible container, such as a bread bowl or hollowed out bell pepper. Dips and spreads also look wonderful in ramekins, colorful soup bowls or large coffee cups. It's a good idea to put a serving spoon into a dip so guests don't have to scoop with a fragile cracker or chip leaving behind broken chunks. They'll also be less likely to "double dip!"

Creamy Dill Veggie Dip (page 140)

Quick Dip

Combine ½ cup prepared ranch dressing and ½ cup prepared salsa for a chunky vegetable dip.

Move Over Potato Chips
Try these different dippers:

Tortilla and potato chips are dandy dippers, but there are plenty of other possibilities, too. Crackers, crisp flat breads, sweet potato chips, bread sticks and melba toast are all excellent options. Vegetables, including the obvious, such as carrot and celery sticks, and the not so obvious, such as green beans, jicama, endive and asparagus, add color and are a healthy addition to a display of dippers. Arranging some dippers vertically in drinking glasses (or vases) adds height and interest.

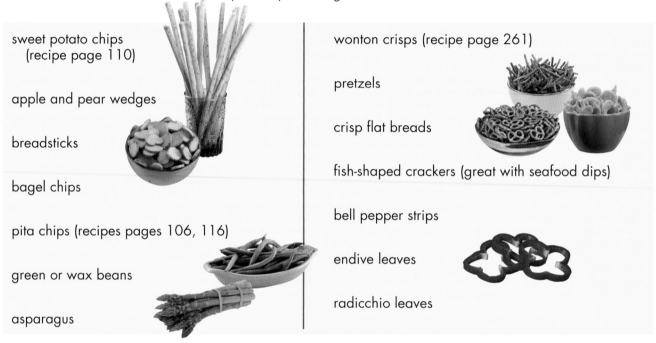

sweet potato chips
  (recipe page 110)

apple and pear wedges

breadsticks

bagel chips

pita chips (recipes pages 106, 116)

green or wax beans

asparagus

wonton crisps (recipe page 261)

pretzels

crisp flat breads

fish-shaped crackers (great with seafood dips)

bell pepper strips

endive leaves

radicchio leaves

How to Rescue a Dip

Dip is too spicy	Add more of a bland ingredient (sour cream, avocado, etc.)
Dip is too runny	If the dip is creamy, add whipped cream cheese. For salsa-type dips, drain excess liquid in a strainer (lined with cheesecloth if necessary)
Dip is too stiff	Call it a spread instead! Or thin with cream, lemon juice, vinegar or mayonnaise
Dip tastes dull	Add lemon or lime juice or a jolt of hot pepper sauce

Kabobs & Their Cousins

Serving an appetizer on a skewer or pick makes it ideal finger food. Every delectable bite comes with a handle! Sticking a frilled toothpick into a cheese cube or melon ball is the simplest form of skewered appetizer, but without much more effort, you can create something new, interesting and even more delicious.

Most every culture has a form of kabob. The cooking method was probably invented centuries ago when hungry Turkish horsemen would skewer pieces of meat on their swords to cook over the fire. Shish kabob is the term used in the Mediterranean. Japan has yakitori skewers, satays are popular Southeast Asian street food and even the French serve food "en brochette." Skewered food not only makes a handy appetizer, it's also a delicious way to combine complementary flavors.

Skewer Pointers

Food cooked on a skewer is usually grilled or broiled. For even cooking, it's important to cut food into uniform pieces. Cooking times need to be kept in mind, too. Don't mix items that take a long time (large chunks of meat) with something that will be overcooked in a matter of minutes (tomatoes).

If you're using bamboo or other wooden skewers, soak them in water for at least 30 minutes before cooking so they won't burn quickly. Position the kabobs so that the wooden handles are away from the hottest portion of the grill or broiler. Cooking ground meat kabob-style is easier if you use a flat-sided skewer and if you refrigerate the meat before cooking so it holds it shape better.

For hors d'oeuvres, it's usually preferable to use wooden skewers rather than metal ones. They will cool more quickly which makes them easier to handle for hot nibbles. Guests can also toss the used skewers instead of worrying about where to put them.

Stuck on Skewers

For bite-size portions, just about anything can be served threaded onto a pick. Meatballs, cheeses and fruit chunks are naturals. Consider spearing small pieces of more expensive treats,

Spicy Thai Satay Dip (page 136)

No-Cook Appetizer Skewers

melon balls with prosciutto wrapped around and between

small fresh mozzarella balls with grape tomatoes and basil leaves

deli chicken cubes with mango or papaya pieces

cooked shrimp with pineapple chunks and mint leaves

pound cake squares and strawberries with chocolate dipping sauce

sharp Cheddar cheese cubes with apple and/or pear wedges

thinly sliced ham wrapped around asparagus pieces

figs or dates, spread with soft cheese and wrapped in slices of ham or prosciutto

sun-dried tomatoes and fresh mozzarella balls rolled in chopped parsley

such as meat or fish, in individual portions to increase the number of servings. Cubes of grilled beef sirloin, coconut shrimp and squares of seared tuna all make elegant eating easy when they're skewered.

Don't limit yourself to plain ordinary toothpicks. You can find hors d'oeuvre picks decorated with sea shells, hearts, glass beads and much more. Asian markets and cooking supply stores stock different lengths of bamboo skewers and often have unusual toothpicks as well. Pretzels make edible handles for cheese or other soft food. Breadsticks can be wrapped with thinly sliced meat or cheese. Even woody-stemmed herbs, such as rosemary, can serve as a skewer (and perfume the food at the same time).

Serving Kabobs and Skewers

Make your kabobs or skewers easy to eat by arranging the handle parts where they're easy to grasp. Longer kabobs can be arranged vertically in a tall container. You can also treat a large vegetable or fruit as a base. Press the pointy end of skewers into a half head of lettuce or a slice of melon to make a porcupine-style display. Make sure there's a place for your guests to either discard or set aside used skewers. If food will be awkward to remove from the kabob stick, supply a plate and fork. Better yet, do as they do in most regions where kabobs are popular. Provide soft pieces of bread to help slide the ingredients off while absorbing the juices.

Sticky Situations

Food slides around on the skewer	Secure food with two skewers, one on each side, instead of just one in the middle
Cooked food sticks to the skewer	Rub the skewer with oil before spearing the ingredients, or invest in nonstick kabob holders
Ingredients take different times	Make separate skewers of ingredients that cook in the same time, or cut ingredients into smaller or larger pieces to even out cooking times. You can also precook items, such as potatoes, in the microwave oven to give them a head start

Beyond Cheese and Crackers

Cheese is a miraculous food with a long history. Experts speculate that humans have been making cheese for more than 12,000 years. There are thousands of cheeses available from every part of the world with hundreds of different flavors and textures. Before you decide you don't want to take the time to learn about such a complex subject, consider the simple fact that all cheese is nothing more than milk in another form. A basic understanding of the types of cheese and a few tips on how to serve them will help you enjoy cheese more and use it in delicious new ways. And you won't have to learn an exotic new language or master a lot of complicated details.

Types of Cheese

It is amazing that the simple process of preserving milk can produce so many luscious variations. While most familiar cheeses are made from cow's milk, cheese is also produced from sheep's milk, goat's milk, buffalo's milk and even yak's milk (not available at your average supermarket!). One way to categorize cheese, then, is by which milk was used to make it. You've probably tasted goat cheese, which is often called by its French name, chèvre. Mozzarella di bufala is made from water buffalo milk and imported from Italy. Creamy, fresh mozzarella made in the United States is from cow's milk. Two popular sheep's milk cheeses you may have sampled are Roquefort and Pecorino Romano.

The other useful way to categorize cheese is based on its moisture content and/or its age.

Fresh cheeses are those that are not aged or processed. Curds are separated from the water-like whey and drained. (In fact, you can make a fresh cheese at home by adding lemon juice to heated milk and watching the curds form, then draining them in cheesecloth or a coffee filter overnight in the refrigerator.) There is no rind, no mold and moisture content is around 80%. Cottage cheese, cream cheese and fresh mozzarella are examples.

Can You Eat the Rind?

The white "bloom" (croute-fleurie or flowering crust in French) on Brie, Camembert and similar cheeses can and should be eaten. Yes, it is a mold, usually a species of penicillin, but relax. It's a natural, edible part of the cheese. Since Brie and Camembert ripen from the outside in, if you skip the rind you could be missing the ripest, tastiest part.

Soft, creamy cheeses have a silky texture and retain 50 to 75% of their moisture. Brie and St. André are examples. Some are characterized as double crème or triple crème, which indicates that cream was added to the milk in the cheese making process. **Semisoft cheeses** have a 40 to 50% moisture content. They are usually mild in flavor. Brick, Jack, Havarti and Gouda are typical cheeses in this category.

Firm cheeses are usually aged, often for years. Cheddar is undoubtedly the favorite firm cheese for eating out of hand. Parmesan and Romano are more often grated and sprinkled over pasta or other dishes. High quality examples of all these cheeses, especially Reggiano Parmesan and Pecorino Romano, are also excellent choices for the cheese board.

Cheese products are important appetizer ingredients. **Process cheese** is made by combining lots of different cheeses with emulsifiers so that it heats evenly and smoothly. **Cheese spreads** and **cold pack cheeses** are generally sold in glass or plastic jars and are flavored. Port wine and garlic and herb spreads are two examples. See the chart (pages 28–29) for additional information.

Storing and Serving Cheese

Unopened cheese can be safely refrigerated in its original wrapper until the freshness date on the package. Artisanal cheeses and those purchased by the piece from gourmet shops are best when served soon after you buy them. Check with the seller as to the best storage for a particular cheese. Cheese is a living thing. Aging contributes to the flavor of many cheeses, but it is aging in a carefully controlled environment, not your refrigerator. Wrap semisoft, firm and hard cheeses tightly. Refrigerated, most will remain fresh for four weeks. Fresh cheeses are higher in moisture, which makes them more perishable. They should be used within two weeks after opening the package. While it is possible to freeze some hard cheeses for up to three months, the flavor and texture will be compromised.

As part of an appetizer buffet, cheese is always a welcome addition. Choose a variety—some creamy, some firm, some sharp, some mild. A buffet is not the place for a very strong smelling cheese, even if it does taste delicious. Instead, save it for a cheese course after a meal or a cheese tasting party. The most important rule is to serve cheese at room temperature so the rich, subtle flavors can be appreciated. Take it out of the refrigerator at least

30 minutes before serving time, longer for big chunks of dense cheese.

Cutting a cheese into portions before serving may be necessary at a large gathering where it's impractical to allow everyone to serve themselves. However, even a firm Cheddar will dry out quickly if it is cut into cubes too far ahead. Keep it wrapped until the last minute and protect it with a glass cover (sometimes called a cheese dome), if possible.

There are dozens of fancy gadgets for cutting cheese; most of them aren't worth bothering with unless you're going to become a connoisseur. Do provide a separate knife for each cheese on your board that needs to be cut. Short-handled servers with wide blades are best for soft cheeses; hard cheeses need sharper knives. Standard steak knives often work well.

Crackers, Grapes and Other Good Matches

To go with a cheese assortment the obvious choices are crackers, crusty breads and, of course, grapes and wine! Many other foods enhance the flavors of cheese, too. A salty cheese, such as Parmesan or Asiago, marries well with a taste of something sweet. Fresh or dried fruit, especially pears, apples and figs go well. Chutney or a good quality fruit preserve served alongside is a nice touch, too. For a

contrast in texture, serve a bowl of nuts or some crisp carrot or celery sticks with your cheese assortment.

To accompany flavorful cheeses, it's best to choose crackers or breads that won't compete. Water crackers are an example of a crisp, bland cracker that will work with most any cheese.

Do You Fondue?

Fondues lend themselves to informal entertaining, so dust off that fondue set you got as a wedding gift and put it to use. If you didn't receive one (horrors!), don't despair. A slow cooker or even an improvised arrangement of an ovenproof container perched over a candle can work. The trick to a smooth fondue is adding the cheese slowly a little at a time over low heat and keeping it warm. Too high a temperature will cause the cheese to separate; too low and it will harden. Fondue is normally served with bread dippers, but crisp tart apples, mushrooms, blanched asparagus, cauliflower and broccoli are nice additions.

For more ideas see Chapter 4, "Cheese, Please" (pages 150–181).

Cheese Chat

cheesemonger: an expert who sells (and knows a lot about) specialty cheeses

cheese dome: a glass cover to place over a platter of cheese to keep it from drying out

artisanal cheese: cheese handcrafted by a small producer

cheesecloth: lightweight cotton gauze fabric used to make cheese (and handy for other kitchen chores, too)

cheese course: an array of cheeses served after the main course (often in place of dessert)

cheese plane: a tool with an inset blade that skims across the surface of a hard cheese to slice it

cheese flight: a group of cheeses from the same category served together so flavor nuances can be appreciated (no cheese plane required!)

POPULAR CHEESES

CHEESE TYPE	CHARACTERISTICS
AMERICAN	a mild Cheddar-type processed cheese; often sold sliced
ASIAGO	an Italian-style hard cheese; mild and buttery when young; Asiago becomes sharp and tangy with aging
BLUE-VEINED	a class of sharp, creamy or crumbly cheeses injected with (friendly) bacteria to create blue or green veins. Maytag blue, French Roquefort and English Stilton are blue-veined
BRICK	a truly American semisoft cheese; originally made in 1870 by pressing into a box-like shape with a brick which gave the cheese its name
BRIE	flat rounds of ultra-rich, creamy cheese with edible white rind; mildly tangy; creamy to runny in texture at room temperature
CAMEMBERT	a classic French cheese from cow's milk; creamy with an edible gray-white rind
CHEDDAR	a firm, white to orange cheese with a mild to sharp flavor, depending on aging; named after an English village
CHÈVRE	tangy, mild and creamy; with age the flavor becomes stronger and the texture drier; chèvre means goat in French
COLBY	a Wisconsin variation on Cheddar; mild and sweet; lighter, softer and more open-textured than Cheddar
COTTAGE CHEESE	a fresh cheese made from whole, low-fat or skim milk
CREAM CHEESE	smooth, spreadable, unripened fresh cheese; Neufchâtel is a lower-fat version
EDAM	yellow cheese from Holland with a red wax coating; semisoft with a mellow, nutty flavor
EMMENTALER	buttery-yellow firm cheese from Switzerland; sweet, nutty flavor
FARMER'S CHEESE	fresh soft cheese similar to dry curd cottage cheese
FETA	brine-cured goat's milk cheese; crumbly, tangy and salty

POPULAR CHEESES

CHEESE TYPE	CHARACTERISTICS
GOUDA	Dutch straw-colored semisoft cheese; mild when young, but sharper with age; often in red wax coating
GRUYÈRE	dry, firm Swiss cheese with a nutty taste and aroma; semisoft with small holes; usually aged
HAVARTI	rich, creamy semisoft Danish cheese; mild when young; often flavored with dill weed or caraway
LIMBURGER	a cow's milk cheese, famous for its pungent aroma; the strong flavor is an acquired taste
MASCARPONE	soft, creamy Italian cheese; often used in desserts, such as tiramisu
MONTEREY JACK	mild, buttery semisoft cheese from Monterey, California; sometimes flavored with jalapeño peppers (pepper jack)
MOZZARELLA	factory-produced mozzarella is semisoft and chewy; fresh mozzarella, available in various size balls is soft and milky-tasting; mozzarella di bufala is a highly prized product made from water buffalo's milk
MUENSTER/ MUNSTER	American Muenster is pale yellow with very small holes and a mild flavor; European Munster is quite pungent
PARMESAN	hard Italian cheese aged to a dry, crumbly texture; flavor is pleasantly sharp and salty; imported Reggiano Parmesan is the standard of excellence
PROVOLONE	mild, slightly smoky, firm Italian cheese; often in a pear shape
RICOTTA	a fresh, white Italian cheese with a sweet mellow taste; similar to cottage cheese
ROMANO/ PECORINO ROMANO	Italian hard cheese from sheep's milk; pungent flavor; often used for grating
SWISS	generic term for a group of pale yellow cheeses with large holes; mild, nutty flavor, slightly dry texture; American Swiss is milder than Emmentaler and Gruyère

Seafood Starters

*Smoked Salmon Lavash
(page 282)*

Many traditional appetizers are based on fish and shellfish. Shrimp cocktail and smoked salmon are two obvious examples. Seafood is flavorful and not too filling so it can tantalize the taste buds and yet still leave room for the main course.

Smoking Allowed

Smoked fish, especially smoked salmon, is a natural for appetizers. Check the refrigerated deli or seafood case in your supermarket. Many ethnic grocers carry a wider array of different kinds of smoked fish as well. You will often find smoked trout, smoked herring and other affordable options. In addition to being a treat served simply with a lemon or dill garnish, smoked fish can be made into a dip or used as a topping for canapés.

Smoked salmon goes by many different names depending on how it is cured and which country is naming it. Lox is brine-cured, cold smoked salmon and a favorite served with bagels and cream cheese. Nova (short for Nova Scotia) salmon is cold-smoked and generally a bit less salty than lox.

Scotch-smoked, Danish-smoked and Irish-smoked salmon refer to smoked Atlantic salmon. Gravlax is a delicious Swedish salt-sugar-dill-cured salmon. All types are generally sliced very thin and paired with dark breads, capers and lemon. See the recipe for Smoked Salmon Lavash (page 282).

Tuna Tips

Tuna is an affordable and tasty hors d'oeuvre ingredient, too. Turned into a dip or a filling for a bite-size pastry, ordinary canned tuna takes on an elegance that goes way beyond tuna salad. Don't forget the many fish choices now available in pouches as well as cans, including flavored versions. Once opened, a can or pouch of tuna should be refrigerated in a sealed container (not the original can or pouch) and used up within 3 to 4 days.

Coming Out of That Shell

Shellfish is a broad, general category that includes all creatures who are supported by a shell on the outside instead of a skeleton on the inside.

It includes shrimp, crab, clams, mussels, scallops, squid and many more. (Even snails are considered shellfish, since they have a shell on the outside!) Cooking with shellfish can seem intimidating because of lack of familiarity. A basic understanding is all you need to start enjoying some of the culinary wonders hidden deep inside those shells.

Buying fresh shellfish is fairly foolproof if you purchase from a reputable fish market or a knowledgeable seafood department in a supermarket with a rapid turnover. All seafood should have a mild aroma and smell of the sea without any strong fishy odor. Bivalves, such as clams, mussels and oysters, should be alive with closed, uncracked shells. It's normal for shells to open slightly from time to time, but they should close when tapped. If they do not close, discard them.

Buy fresh shellfish the same day you plan to serve it.

Shellfish need to be stored in a cold, moist environment. Keep them in the coldest part of your refrigerator (usually the top shelf). Live shellfish need to breath, so never put them in an airtight container or in fresh water. Instead, store them in a shallow dish covered with a damp towel.

Shrimp and shucked clams or oysters may be kept in a leakproof bag or covered container.

Frozen shellfish need careful handling, too. Store them in a home freezer for no more than six months. The longer the storage, the greater the loss of flavor and texture. Always thaw frozen seafood in the refrigerator rather than at room temperature. If you need to thaw shrimp faster, place the crustaceans in a colander and run cold water over them, separating them to speed the process.

Shellfish Safety

Shellfish are low in fat and high in both protein and beneficial omega-3 fatty acids. Unfortunately, it is also true that eating raw shellfish can be a risky business. It causes more illnesses than eating all other fish combined. It goes without saying that buying shellfish from a reputable source is of paramount importance. All legally fished clams and oysters are from licensed, inspected areas and are tagged with this information. Many people are also allergic to shellfish. At a party, it is wise to label any dip or hors d'oeuvre that contains it, so those with sensitivities may easily avoid it.

Shrimp Cocktail and Other Delights

When it comes to shellfish, shrimp is far and away the favorite. Few appetizers are easier or more appreciated than shrimp cocktail.

Awww, shucks!

The easiest way to get to the meat inside a clam or oyster is to steam it just until the shell opens. Shucking raw bivalves is trickier, but here's how:

To shuck a clam: Insert a sturdy paring knife opposite the hinge to pry open the clam.

To shuck an oyster: Place the oyster on a flat surface or hold it wrapped in a kitchen towel to protect your hands. Holding the deep side of the shell down, insert the point of an oyster knife into the hinge between the shells at the oyster's pointed end and twist. Once the hinge muscle is cut, run the knife between the shells to open.

Oysters Romano (page 54)

Shrimp Dip with Crudités (page 138)

Buying the shrimp is actually the most complicated part of the task.

Shrimp is extremely perishable and freezes well, so virtually all of it is frozen where it is caught and shipped that way. The bins of "fresh" shrimp at the market most likely were thawed on the premises (hopefully, on the same day they are being sold). You can purchase frozen shrimp either cooked or raw. While pre-cooked, peeled shrimp is slightly more convenient, it tends to have a less firm texture and blander flavor than shrimp you cook in the shell. One pound of raw shrimp should yield about six appetizer servings. That's four or five large shrimp per person.

Many recipes call for peeling and deveining shrimp. (The "vein" is actually an intestinal tract. It's not harmful to eat, but can be gritty or bitter on large shrimp. There's no need to devein small or medium shrimp.) Some frozen raw shrimp, usually labeled "easy peel," has been deveined for you. To do it yourself, make a shallow cut along the back of the shrimp and lift out the dark vein with the tip of a knife. You may find the job easier if it is done under cold running water.

Cocktail sauce can be store-bought or homemade or something in between. Try adding fresh herbs or a bit of fresh lemon juice to your favorite brand to brighten its flavor. If you're planning a big get-together and shrimp cocktail is too expensive a proposition for a crowd, try one of the other appetizer recipes using shrimp, such as Shrimp Dip with Crudités (page 138) or Grilled Antipasto Platter (page 176).

Yields Per Pound of Shrimp

Jumbo: 11–15 shrimp

Extra-large: 16–20 shrimp

Large: 21–30 shrimp

Medium: 31–35 shrimp

Small: 36–45 shrimp

Shellfish Types	Sold in These Forms	Varieties Available
Bivalves (two shells)		
clams	fresh (live in shell), shucked and packed with their own liquid, canned (chopped or whole)	hard shell: littlenecks, cherrystones, chowder clams (quahogs); soft-shell: steamer clams, razor clams
oysters	fresh (live in shell), shucked and packed in their own liquid, canned (smoked)	Eastern, Pacific, European flat, Kumamoto (other names, such as bluepoint, are references to growing regions)
scallops	fresh (shucked), frozen (plain or breaded)	calico, sea, bay
mussels	fresh (live in shells)	blue, New Zealand green-lipped
Cephalopods (with tentacles)		
squid (calamari)	fresh (rarely), frozen: whole or breaded pieces	short-finned, long-finned, cuttlefish
octopus	fresh (rarely), frozen	
Crustaceans (jointed shells)		
lobster	fresh (live in shell), frozen (tails)	Maine, spiny
shrimp	"fresh" (usually means recently thawed), frozen (raw or cooked),	white, pink, black, tiger
crab	fresh (live in shell), fresh (picked from shell), pasteurized (refrigerated) canned	King, Dungeness, blue, snow

Fruit & Veggie Bites

Dreamy Orange Cheesecake Dip (page 156)

The produce aisle (or better yet, a farmer's market or your own garden) is a great place to gather the makings for appetizers. Fresh fruit and vegetables add color, texture and variety to any hors d'oeuvre assortment or buffet table. They also create healthy options that are welcome to anyone with dietary restrictions.

It may seem obvious, but the best thing you can do to serve tasty fruits and vegetables is to purchase the right ones. This means choosing in-season produce from a reputable source.

Where possible, pick fresh fruits and vegetables that are grown close to home since they are likely to have had more time to ripen naturally. Frozen products are usually excellent year-round and a good substitute for fresh when you will be cooking with them or using them as an ingredient. If you're short on time, look for prewashed greens, pre-cut broccoli florets and the like in the refrigerated section. For a small amount of a particular item, the salad bar can be a good choice.

From Apricot to Watermelon

One of the most beloved appetizers in Italian cuisine is the simplest to make: prosciutto wrapped around a slice of perfectly ripe melon. The sweetness of the fruit pairs perfectly with the slightly salty ham. Most fruit also works well with spicy flavors, as in salsa. Creamy concoctions made with fruit are delightful, too. It's hard to beat a strawberry cream cheese spread or apricot Brie.

It seems as if fruit goes with almost everything!

A platter piled with fresh fruit is a simple-to-make, hard-to-resist offering. Keep the pieces large and arrange them in groups. Some fruit is best served whole, such as strawberries and cherries (leave the stems on, if possible). Slices of watermelon, fresh pineapple, pear wedges and small bunches of grapes look gorgeous tucked around and between. Vary the colors and shapes to make a pleasing pattern based on what's available and what looks pretty. Fruit also looks beautiful arranged on bamboo skewers, like miniature kabobs. To keep cut fruits, such as apples and pears, from browning when exposed to the air, rub the surfaces with the cut edges of a lemon or lime.

Fresh fruit is even more appealing when a dip is offered alongside. It can be as simple as a bowl of brown sugar and another of sour cream. For something fancier, see the recipe for Curried Fruit Dip (page 122). Chocolate-dipped fruit pieces look elegant but are surprisingly easy to make. (See the sidebar for the recipe.) Dip some dried apricots, nuts or pretzels in chocolate, too, while you're at it, for a sweet bite everyone will love.

Tropical Treats

Now that mangoes and kiwi have become mainstream, take advantage of their abundance and their gaudy colors. Fresh pineapple is readily available and the new varieties (usually marketed as "gold") are wonderfully sweet. For a truly exotic fruit platter, look for some of the newer imports becoming available. Star fruit (carambola) looks like its name and makes a beautiful garnish cut into star-shaped slices. Pomegranates are in season in the fall. Their jewel-like seeds look stunning scattered over a dip or fruit platter.

Vegetables on Their Own: Crudités

A crudité platter is almost an appetizer cliché—an arrangement of carrot and celery sticks with some broccoli florets

Louisiana Crap Dip with Crudités (page 144)

Chocolate-Dipped Fruit

½ cup semisweet chocolate chips

1 teaspoon shortening

Assorted fresh fruit, cut into bite-size pieces

1. Place chocolate chips and shortening in small microwavable bowl. Microwave at HIGH 1½ to 3 minutes or until smooth when stirred, stirring after each minute. (Or, place in top of double boiler. Heat over boiling water until chocolate is smooth when stirred.)

2. Dip fruit pieces into chocolate. Place on waxed paper-lined baking sheet; let stand until chocolate is set.

Blanching Vegetables

Fill a large saucepan halfway with water, add a teaspoon of salt and bring to a boil. Meanwhile, fill a large bowl with ice water. Blanch vegetables with the same amount of cooking time in batches and make sure there's plenty of rapidly boiling water so they move around freely and cook evenly. Boil each batch for about 1 minute. To stop the cooking and preserve color, quickly remove the vegetables with a slotted spoon or tongs and immediately plunge them into the ice water. Drain well and refrigerate them until serving time.

and tomatoes for color. (The French word "crudité" simply means raw.) To make raw vegetables a more inspiring and better tasting appetizer, choose seasonal produce and plenty of it. It's much better to have fewer selections in a larger quantity than to fill a platter with mediocre specimens. How vegetables are prepared and arranged makes a difference, too. If it seems that broccoli florets always get left behind on the platter at parties, that's because raw broccoli is not very appealing and is hard to digest. Many vegetables (broccoli, cauliflower, asparagus) look and taste better if they've been blanched first. See the sidebar for simple directions.

Adding some new choices to a crudités selection can make it more interesting. Consider jicama, snow peas, red pepper strips, yellow squash, endive leaves or yellow wax beans. Arrange some items vertically in glasses or jars to add height. See Chapter 3, "Dips and Spreads" (pages 116–149) for suggestions on what to serve with your vegetable platter.

Veggies to Stuff and Stack

Slices of cucumber, zucchini and even radish are natural bases for canapés. Try them instead of bread topped with a dip or spread. For a special effect, use a pastry bag to make a decorative

Zucchini Pizza Bites (page 100)

swirl. It's not as difficult as you might think. In fact, it's almost as easy as spreading a topping with a knife once you get the knack.

Some vegetables are perfect for stuffing. Hollow out cherry tomatoes with a small sharp knife and cut a tiny slice off the bottom so they won't roll around. Fill with a creamy dip or a bit of crumbled cheese or some seafood salad. (A pastry bag helps here, too.) Cooked small red potatoes can be handled in much the same way.

Patrician Escargots (page 52)

Stuffed mushrooms are popular hors d'oeuvres for good reason. Their round dish-like shape, earthy flavor and sturdy texture make perfect finger food. See the recipe for Crab and Artichoke Stuffed Mushrooms (page 186). For stuffing, choose fresh, unblemished mushrooms (white button or brown cremini) that are big enough to stuff, but not too big to eat in a few bites.

Doing the Dip

Instead of serving vegetables with a dip, why not make a dip with vegetables? Hummus, a Middle Eastern specialty made from chick-peas, has become so popular you can purchase it already prepared at almost any supermarket. It's also incredibly easy to make at home. (See the recipe on page 136.) Spinach and artichoke dip are all-time favorites, too, and there are hot and cold versions to suit every palate. And bean dip is on every TV table at Super Bowl time.

Hot Artichoke Dip (page 126)

Mushrooms: To Rinse or Wipe?

There are endless opinions on this subject. Vehement voices on the side of wiping claim that cleaning with water makes mushrooms soggy. There are even special mushroom brushes sold to do the job. It is true that mushrooms absorb liquid like little sponges and should never be soaked. On the other hand, a quick rinse under running water won't hurt and can make cleaning dirty mushrooms faster and easier.

Using a Pastry Bag

Cloth or plastic pastry bags and the tips that go with them are available at cookware shops. For filling and decorating hors d'oeuvres, you only need basic tips (a straight tip and a star tip should do it.) The easiest way to fill a pastry bag is to set it vertically, tip down, in a tall glass. Fold the edge of the bag down over the glass and scoop the filling into the bag. Do not fill it more than halfway.

To pipe a filling, unfold the cuff and gather the edge of the bag together. Use one hand to twist the top of the bag and push the filling towards the tip. Your other hand should be lower on the bag to gently squeeze and guide the filling out of the tip. Practice a few times on a piece of waxed paper until you get a feel for the technique. Pastry bags are useful for filling or decorating all sorts of appetizers.

Caviar and Pâté on a Budget

Few folks can afford to buy beluga caviar for a party. And it's just as well. Imported caviar is not to everyone's taste and, as of this writing, beluga sturgeon caviar from the Black Sea is restricted from import because sturgeon are endangered.

If you want to capture the flavor and mystique of caviar, there are plenty of alternatives. Supermarkets carry jarred lumpfish caviar in red and black that can provide some of caviar's pizzazz for small change. Try serving lumpfish caviar with sour cream and crêpes. (See the crêpe recipe on page 293.) You'll be recreating a famous Russian hors d'oeuvre, caviar and blini. Blini are pancakes made with buckwheat, but regular crêpes are easier to make and just as delicious. If fish eggs are not your thing, try Cowboy Caviar (page 130), made from black-eyed peas, or Eggplant Caviar (page 309).

Pâté: Liver Sausage with a Fancy Name

Sshhh! Don't let the French hear you. Pâté simply means "pie" in French and is usually used to refer to an elegant mixture of ground poultry or meat with seasonings cooked in a mold and served as an appetizer. The most famous (and horrendously expensive) example is pâté de foie gras, which is made from goose liver. Pâté can be much more modest and can be made from many ingredients. The Jewish-American favorite chopped liver is one example. Liver isn't a required ingredient either, and making a pâté need not be complicated. See the recipe for Zesty Liver Pâté (page 282) for a classic but simple version.

Cowboy Caviar (page 130)

The word "terrine" originally referred to the mold a pâté was cooked in. Now it has come to mean the dish that is served as well as the cooking vessel. While you can purchase special terrine molds shaped like ducks or rabbits, you can also prepare a terrine in an ordinary loaf pan with good results. The Elegant Pork Terrine shown on the right is an example of using this technique.

While pâté and terrine are terms that are used interchangeably, terrine more often refers to an appetizer composed in layers and served in slices to reveal a mosaic-like interior of different ingredients. They can be made of ground meat or fish and layered with brightly colored vegetables. Sometimes they are studded with pistachios, olives and other ingredients. Although a terrine may look fancy, when you come right down to it, it's really a meat loaf!

What To Serve with Pâtés and Terrines

A cost-conscious hostess or host can easily stretch an elegant appetizer by serving an array of appropriate accompaniments. Crusty bread, crisp crackers or toasts are necessities. For rich hors d'oeuvres, sweet or salty flavors work well. Cornichons (those tiny pickles you often see served with pâté) are a good example. They can usually be purchased in the supermarket pickle aisle and are really nothing more than baby gherkins. If you can't find cornichons, try another small, tart pickle. A good quality Dijon mustard is another must-have with pâté. Fruit preserves, chutneys or fruit compotes contrast nicely with rich meat-based offerings. A tart vegetable salad made with shredded carrot or cabbage can also be a welcome go-with.

Elegant Pork Terrine (page 62)

Shrimp Pâté

  ½ pound cooked peeled shrimp
  ¼ cup (½ stick) unsalted butter, cut into chunks
  2 teaspoons dry vermouth or chicken broth
  1 teaspoon *each* lemon juice and Dijon mustard
  ¼ teaspoon *each* salt and ground mace
  ⅛ teaspoon *each* ground red pepper and black pepper
  ½ cup chopped pistachio nuts
  2 large heads Belgian endive

Combine shrimp, butter, vermouth, lemon juice, mustard, salt, mace, red pepper and black pepper in blender or food processor. Process until smooth. If mixture is too soft to handle, refrigerate 1 hour. Spread pistachio nuts on sheet of waxed paper. Gently shape shrimp mixture into 8-inch log. Roll in nuts to coat. Chill 1 to 3 hours. Separate endive into individual leaves and serve with shrimp log.

A World of Appetizers

Favorite Mexican Appetizers

guacamole

salsa

nachos

quesadillas

sopes

tortilla roll-ups

Favorite French Appetizers

baked Brie

canapés

cheese

crêpes

escargot (snails)

pâté

terrines

Every culture and cuisine has its own interpretation of appetizers. Spain has tapas bars. Italy is famous for antipasti, China for dim sum. The Middle East has meze and France is the home of hors d'oeuvres. Many of the traditions and recipes overlap and have influenced one another. Virtually every cuisine has a form of dumpling, from Polish pierogi to Latin American empanadas. Then there are the dips, breads, spreads, kabobs, relishes and chutneys that go by many different names and display a multitude of wonderful flavors. Here is a very brief tour of the international world of appetizers.

Guacamole Olé

South-of-the-border appetizers have become such American favorites we hardly think of them as ethnic anymore. What would a Super Bowl party be without guacamole? Nachos are everywhere, including schools, bars and airports. Mexican munchies are so versatile and so delicious it's easy to forget that they were "foreign" food

Classic Guacamole (page 58)

not that long ago. Strong flavors, bright colors and plenty of fresh fruit and vegetables dominate these appetizers. There's something about sharing Mexican nibbles that always creates a fiesta mood.

Pass the Pâté, S'il Vous Plait

The French invented the language of appetizers—hors d'oeuvre, canapé, pâté, terrine. They're responsible for some of our most elegant and traditional small plates. French flavors are balanced and surprising. Who'd guess that a pickle would go so well with a liver pâté? And who but the French could add garlic and parsley to the humble snail and turn it into haute cuisine? Appetizers are the perfect place to enjoy the rich, luxurious flavors of French cuisine in small, digestible bites.

Antipasti and Tapas

Italy and Spain have a long tradition of serving delightful appetizers. Maybe it's the warm climate, or the warm people, but Italians and Spaniards seem to relish sitting down with a glass of wine and a plate of nibbles. No wonder there are so many

Tomato and Caper Crostini (page 98)

popular recipes based on these cuisines.

Antipasto (plural antipasti) literally means "before the meal" and includes cold or hot food. Cold antipasti are most often platters of cured meats, such as prosciutto and salami, plus cheese, olives and marinated vegetables. A hot antipasto can be anything from shrimp scampi to pizza. Most antipasti are served with good crusty bread and, naturally, some "vino."

Spanish tapas are traditionally bar snacks—small plates of something tasty to accompany drinks. The word tapas means "cover." Originally a saucer (or a slice of bread) was used to cover drinks to protect them from flies. Bartenders began placing a little snack for their patrons on top of the saucer and tapas were born. Traditional tapas include olives, omelets, seafood and roasted peppers.

Mediterranean Meze

From Istanbul to Athens, the Mediterranean region has a strong tradition of serving an array of appetizers in the middle of the day to go along with conversation and drinks. In fact, the word meze means "middle of the day." Meze (also spelled mezze and meza) are often snacks served between lunch and dinner, but there

Favorite Antipasti and Tapas

bruschetta

calamari

caponata

crostini

pizza

prosciutto, salami and cured meats

roasted red peppers

shrimp scampi

tortellini

Favorite Mediterranean Appetizers

hummus

meatballs

falafel

phyllo triangles (spanakopita)

grilled feta

olives

stuffed grape leaves

Favorite Asian Appetizers

dim sum dumplings

egg rolls, spring and summer rolls

peanut dip

pot stickers

samosas

satay

tempura

wontons

Falafel with Garlic Tahini Sauce (page 250)

Southeast Asia brings us the appetizer called satay (or saté), a grilled skewer of meat, fish or poultry often served with peanut sauce. Japan offers tempura, deep-fried batter-dipped fish and vegetables. India's version of the dumpling is the luscious samosa, a triangular packet of dough filled with spicy vegetables or meat. From dim sum to samosas, these finger foods are always served with a dipping sauce and a large portion of hospitality.

Apricot-Chicken Pot Stickers (page 262)

are really no rules about when these tasty tidbits can be enjoyed. Meze include Greek spanakopita (phyllo triangles), Middle Eastern hummus and falafel and much more.

Dim Sum and Then Some

China is famous for dim sum, little bites of delicious food served with tea, including dumplings, rice balls, pot stickers and pastries. Dim sum means "heart's delight" and can be served any time of day. Egg rolls, summer rolls and spring rolls are all Asian treats that involve dough wrapped around a savory filling in a roll-shape, kind of like a long, thin dumpling.

Serving with Style

Eyes taste before mouths do, and this is especially true in the case of appetizers. Imagine a bag of chips set out with salsa still in the plastic tub from the grocery store versus a napkin-lined basket of home-style chips next to an earthenware bowl filled with dip and garnished with fresh cilantro. Which would be more likely to make mouths water?

Presentation is important, but there's no need to learn to carve a peacock out of a watermelon or spend a fortune on new serving dishes. A little thoughtful creativity goes a very long way. Pleasing yourself and expressing your own personal style is better than trying to copy someone else's. Adapt ideas to suit your particular guest list, serving dishes, budget and space limitations.

Think Outside the Bowl

Take a look around your house (not just the kitchen, either) with eyes wide open and you may find new ways to serve ordinary appetizers. Dip doesn't have to be in a bowl—what about a giant coffee cup or an oversized martini glass? Baskets can hold bread, chips, crackers and the like. Lined with with a napkin or piece of fabric, even baskets with an open weave or those meant to be purely decorative will work. You can put souvenir dishes, cleaned shells from the beach or those ceramics your kid made at camp to use, too. A bamboo steamer filled with hors d'oeuvres looks lovely even if they weren't actually steamed. Cutting boards, marble tiles, mirrors or picture frames can be pressed into service as trays. Small bites can be arranged in spoons or on coasters.

Timing is Everything

If appetizers are being served buffet-style, it's important to plan how you will keep platters neat and filled. Nothing looks sadder than a single tired canapé on a large plate of wilted lettuce. Keep extra food hot in the oven or cold in the refrigerator until you're ready to serve it. This keeps food at safe temperatures for a longer period. It's better, quicker and safer to replace empty platters with full ones rather than trying to add to an existing dish. Think ahead about the logistics of baking hot appetizers. You'll want to time them so they're ready in stages throughout the party. And don't forget to take the cheese out of the refrigerator at least 30 minutes before you want to serve it.

Garnish Is Your Friend

The best time to think about garnish is before you prepare the recipe. Often the most appropriate garnish is an ingredient you'll be using. Fresh herbs make especially lovely garnishes, but if you chop up all the basil, you won't have a sprig left over. A garnish should ALWAYS be edible. It should look natural and the flavor should work with the food being presented. Don't force things. When in doubt, it's better not to garnish. You should consider how the appetizer will be eaten, too. What's the point in putting a perfect carrot curl on top of a bowl of dip when it will immediately be submerged? On the other hand,

garnish can save a presentation. Did the quiche or poached salmon develop huge cracks? Hide them with an appropriate garnish and no one will be the wiser.

What goes under the food on the platter makes a difference, too. Leafy greens almost always work since they add color and texture. Don't limit it to lettuce, either. Cabbage, kale and chard all come in a range of beautiful, natural colors. Caterers have discovered a trick you can also utilize. They line trays or platters with dried beans, rock salt or chopped red pepper pieces. This looks pretty and can also help keep some appetizers steadier on the platter.

Give Things a Lift

Adding height to some of the dishes on a table adds drama and also makes it easier to see what's displayed. You can easily achieve as many levels as you wish by propping up plates with books, cans or anything else as long as they're covered by a tablecloth or napkin. Footed cake platters make good servers, too, even if there is no cake involved. Arranging bread sticks, asparagus or skewered appetizers in a tall glass or vase also adds dimension.

Buffet Food Safety

1. Keep hot food hot (over 140°F) and cold food cold (under 40°F).

2. Don't leave any perishable food out at room temperature for longer than 2 hours.

3. Replace empty platters with freshly filled ones. Many hands have touched food that is sitting at room temperature and adding more may be unsafe.

4. Discard any food that has sat on the buffet table at room temperature for more than 2 hours.

An Appetizer Glossary

amuse bouche: (pronounced ah-mewz-BOOSH) the French word for a small appetizer that tickles the taste buds (amuses the mouth)

antipasto: the Italian word for hot or cold hors d'oeuvres, usually including cheese, smoked meats, olives, fish and vegetables

artisanal cheese: handmade cheese, produced primarily by small independent cheesemakers using traditional methods

baba ganoush: (pronounced bah-bah gah-NOOSH) a Middle Eastern spread or dip made primarily of eggplant (see recipe for Smoky Eggplant Dip on page 116 for a version)

bivalve: a shellfish that has two shells hinged together, such as a clam, oyster or mussel

blind baking: baking an unfilled pastry shell which will later be filled

blini: Russian-style buckwheat pancakes often served with caviar

bocconcini: (pronounced bohk-kohn-CHEE-nee) small, round balls of fresh mozzarella cheese

bread bowl: a hollowed-out loaf of bread that is used to hold dips, soups or similar foods

bruschetta: (pronounced broo-SKEH-ta) toasted garlic bread served plain or topped with chopped tomato

Buffalo wings: spicy wings usually served with a blue-cheese dipping sauce; named after a bar in Buffalo, New York

calamari: Italian for squid; usually refers to deep-fried breaded squid rings served as an appetizer

canapé: small piece of bread or toast, topped with a spread and/or a garnish

caponata: a Sicilian relish, often served as a spread or dip, made of eggplant, tomato, olives, anchovy, capers and vinegar

caviar: fish eggs (roe); the most expensive caviar comes from sturgeon, but salmon, lumpfish, whitefish and many other varieties are also available

ceviche (also spelled **seviche**)**:** (pronounced seh-VEE-cheh) a Latin American appetizer composed of raw fish "cooked" in citrus juice

cheese flight: a group of cheeses from the same category served together so flavor nuances can be appreciated

chile con queso: (pronounced CHIHL-ee kon KAY-soh) a melted cheese dip flavored with mild green chili peppers

chutney: a spicy-sweet relish of East Indian origin usually made from fruit, vinegar, sugar and spices; mango chutney is one delicious example

cocktail sauce: a combination of ketchup, horseradish and seasonings served with seafood appetizers, usually shrimp cocktail

compound butter: a flavored butter made by adding chopped herbs, shallots or similar ingredients

cornichon: (pronounced KOR-nih-shohn) a tiny, tart pickle (gherkin) often served as an accompaniment with pâté

crème fraîche: (pronounced krehm FRESH) a tangy thickened cream, similar to sour cream; crème fraîche does not curdle with boiling

crêpe: a thin, light pancake, often filled with sweet or savory ingredients

croquette: a mixture of minced meat and/or vegetables, shaped into a patty and fried

crostini: little toasts of bread with a savory topping; the Italian version of canapés

croustade: (pronounced kroo-STAHD) a square of bread, toasted (often in a muffin tin) in the shape of a cup to hold a filling

crudités: (pronounced kroo-dee-TAY) raw vegetables served as an appetizer, usually with a dip

devein: to remove the black vein from the back of a shrimp

dim sum: Chinese dumplings and pastries served with tea in appetizer-size portions

double-crème, triple-crème cheese: soft, creamy cow's milk cheeses that have been enriched with extra cream during production; double crème is at least 60% milk fat; triple crème is at least 75%

drummette: the middle portion of a chicken wing between the wing tip and double bone section; it looks like a tiny drumstick

dumpling: a dough packet stuffed with meat, vegetables or fish; usually steamed or deep-fried

edamame: (pronounced eh-dah-MAH-meh) green soybeans in the pod; available in the freezer case; a popular snack with drinks in Japan

egg roll: a Chinese appetizer consisting of a thin sheet of pastry folded around a savory filling, then deep fried (see **spring roll; summer roll**)

empanada: a Latin American pastry turnover with a savory, or occasionally a sweet, filling

endive: also known as Belgian endive or French endive; a tightly packed cigar-shaped head of cream-colored, slightly bitter leaves, related to chicory and escarole

escargot: French for snail; served with garlic butter, escargot is a classic appetizer

falafel: a Middle Eastern specialty consisting of small, ball-shaped croquettes made of spicy ground chick-peas; usually served with a yogurt-based sauce

finger sandwich: a small appetizer version of a sandwich, often served with tea (see **tea sandwich**)

first course: the appetizer part of a meal; most often part of a formal meal served before the main course

focaccia: (pronounced foh-KAH-chyah) a relatively flat Italian yeast bread often sprinkled with herbs

fondue: a savory or sweet melted mixture kept hot in a special pot and served with bread, vegetables or fruit for dipping; cheese fondue is the most common variety

guacamole: a Mexican sauce or dip made primarily of avocados mashed with lime juice and other seasonings

hummus: (pronounced HOOM-uhs) a Middle Eastern dip made from mashed chick-peas and usually served with pita bread

meze (also spelled **mezze** and **meza**)**:** (pronounced meh-ZAY) Greek for hor d'oeuvres; an assortment of snacks most often served between lunch and dinner in Mediterranean countries

nachos: a Mexican appetizer consisting of crisp tortilla chips topped with cheese, chili peppers and other ingredients

nori: black, paper-thin sheets of seaweed used to wrap **sushi** rolls

pâté: (pronounced pah-TAY) ground meat (often liver), fish, game or vegetables, highly seasoned and baked in a terrine or a pastry crust

pâté de foie gras: (pronounced pah-TAY duh FWAH GRAH) the most expensive and luxurious **pâté** made from goose liver that has been enlarged by force feeding the goose.

pierogi: (pronounced peer-OH-gee) a Polish **dumpling** with a savory or sweet filling, such as sauerkraut, onions, dried fruit or blueberries

pinwheel: refers to an appetizer which is rolled up to form a spiral, then sliced into pieces revealing a pinwheel pattern

pita: a round of flat Middle Eastern bread that can be separated into two layers to form a pocket; wedges of pita (pita chips) are often toasted and used as dippers

pot stickers: small Asian **dumplings** made with **wonton wrappers** and filled with meat, vegetables or seafood; browned on one side so they stick to the pot (hence the name)

prosciutto: (pronounced proh-SHOO-toh) an Italian ham that is pressed, seasoned and cured but not smoked; sold in paper-thin slices

puff: a light, hollow pastry, usually round and often filled

quesadilla: (pronounced keh-sah-DEE yah) a tortilla filled with a savory mixture then folded in half and toasted or fried; cut into wedges or strips as an appetizer

quiche: a pastry shell filled with a savory custard which includes meat, fish or vegetables; often served as an hor d'oeuvre (or as a brunch main course)

radicchio: (pronounced rah-DEE-kee-oh) a dark reddish-purple, slightly bitter form of chicory; leaves are used for appetizer wrappers or as a salad green

relish: a highly seasoned condiment eaten with another food to add flavor

salsa: Spanish for "sauce"; cooked or fresh mixtures of vegetables almost always featuring tomatoes

samosa: East Indian triangular pastry filled with meat and/or vegetables and deep fried; a popular snack and street food

satay: a Southeast Asian skewer of meat, fish or poultry that is grilled or broiled; usually served with peanut sauce

shuck: to remove the shell from oysters or clams (also to peel the husk from an ear of corn)

small plate: an appetizer portion of food served on an individual plate; restaurants sometimes offer a menu of small plates that can be combined to make a meal

sopes: small masa (corn dough) cakes filed with beans, chorizo or other savory fillings

spring roll: a smaller, more delicate version of an egg roll (see **egg roll; summer roll**)

summer roll: a Vietnamese appetizer shaped like an egg roll with a wrapper made of thin, translucent rice paper.

sushi: A Japanese specialty; boiled rice is topped with raw fish for nigiri sushi; for sushi rolls, rice and vegetables or fish are enclosed in a **nori** wrapper

tahini: sesame seed paste; usually an ingredient in **hummus** and **baba ganoush**

tapas: (pronounced TAH-pahs) in Spain, **small plates** usually served at a tapas bar to accompany drinks

tapenade: (pronounced TA-puh-nahd) a Provençal dip or spread made from olives, capers and anchovies

tartlets: miniature appetizer-size pastries

tea sandwich: a small appetizer portion of a sandwich served with tea; usually crustless and often filled with cucumber slices, watercress or other light ingredients (see **finger sandwich**)

tempura: a Japanese specialty of batter-dipped, deep-fried fish and/or vegetables

terrine: the mold a pâté is cooked in; also a pâté, often composed of layers of ground meat, fish or vegetables

toast points: triangular pieces of thinly sliced white bread (one slice yields four points), toasted and used as an appetizer accompaniment or base

torta: Italian for tart, pie or cake; also, Spanish for cake, loaf or sandwich; in both cuisines torta sometimes refers to a terrine-type appetizer

tostada: a crisp-fried tortilla, topped with shredded meat, beans and/or lettuce and tomato

tostones: (pronounced tohs-TOH-nays) savory chips made from plantains (a type of banana); Latin American "chips"

wonton: a bite-size Chinese **dumpling** with a savory filling; wontons may be boiled, steamed or fried

wonton wrapper: a paper-thin piece of dough (square or round) used to wrap **egg rolls** or other appetizers; usually sold in packages in the supermarket freezer case or refrigerated produce section

zakuski: (pronounced zuh-KOOS-kee) a Russian hors d'oeuvre assortment; often includes caviar and ice-cold vodka

Recipes for all the best appetizers, first courses and hors d'oeuvres

You'll find plenty of appetizing ideas in the pages that follow. Recipes for starters, canapés, dips, nibbles and finger food of all kinds come with clear, easy to follow instructions and plenty of color photos of the finished product to inspire you.

Whether you're looking for a simple onion dip or you want to try your hand at making a terrine for the first time, success is practically guaranteed. There are more than 150 recipes including classics, such as crab cakes and deviled eggs, as well as international favorites, including Shrimp Tapas in Sherry Sauce. You'll also find an entire chapter devoted to cheese appetizers and another filled with dozens of recipes for dips and spreads.

Hors d'oeuvres are fun to prepare and delightful to eat because they offer a lot of small tastes of many wonderful flavors. And since they are always made for sharing, appetizers can turn almost any occasion into a party.

Clams Casino (page 74)

Classic Starters

Baked Brie with Nut Crust

⅓ cup pecans
⅓ cup almonds
⅓ cup walnuts
1 egg
1 tablespoon heavy cream
1 wheel (8 ounces) Brie cheese
2 tablespoons raspberry jam

1. Preheat oven to 350°F. Place nuts in food processor fitted with steel blade; pulse to finely chop. *Do not overprocess.* Transfer chopped nuts to shallow dish or pie plate.

2. Combine egg and cream in another shallow dish; whisk until well blended.

3. Dip Brie (rind on) into egg mixture; then into nut mixture, turning to coat. Press nuts to adhere.

4. Transfer Brie to baking sheet; spread jam over top. Bake 15 minutes or until cheese is warm and soft. *Makes 8 servings*

tip

Choose a wheel of Brie that is soft but not overly ripe for this recipe. Overripe Brie is runny and will not hold it's shape. Choose a cheese that is plump and resilient to the touch. Store Brie in the refrigerator wrapped in plastic wrap or foil. If the cheese becomes too runny or smells of ammonia, discard it.

Baked Brie with Nut Crust

Patrician Escargots

½ cup olive oil
½ cup (1 stick) butter
1 onion, finely chopped
2 tablespoons minced garlic
1 teaspoon finely chopped fresh rosemary *or* ½ teaspoon dried
    rosemary
¼ teaspoon dried thyme
2 dashes ground nutmeg
    Salt and black pepper
24 large canned snails, rinsed and drained
½ cup chopped fresh parsley
24 large fresh mushrooms
12 thin slices white bread

1. Heat oil and butter in large skillet over medium heat until butter is melted. Add onion, garlic, rosemary, thyme and nutmeg; season with salt and pepper. Reduce heat to low; add snails and parsley. Cook 30 minutes, stirring occasionally.

2. Preheat oven to 350°F. Remove stems from mushrooms and discard.

3. Arrange mushroom caps upside down in 2-inch-deep baking dish; place 1 snail from garlic mixture in each mushroom cap. Pour garlic mixture over snails; cover with foil and bake 30 minutes.

4. Meanwhile, remove crusts from bread slices. Toast each slice and cut diagonally into 4 triangles. Serve with escargots. *Makes 24 appetizers*

Patrician Escargots

The Famous Lipton® California Dip

**1 envelope LIPTON® RECIPE SECRETS® Onion Soup Mix
1 container (16 ounces) regular or light sour cream**

1. In medium bowl, blend all ingredients; chill at least 2 hours.

2. Serve with your favorite dippers.   *Makes about 2 cups dip*

Tip: For a creamier dip, add more sour cream.

Sensational Spinach Dip: Add 1 package (10 ounces) frozen chopped spinach, thawed and squeezed dry.

California Seafood Dip: Add 1 cup finely chopped cooked clams, crabmeat or shrimp, ¼ cup chili sauce and 1 tablespoon horseradish.

California Bacon Dip: Add ⅓ cup crumbled cooked bacon or bacon bits.

California Blue Cheese Dip: Add ¼ pound crumbled blue cheese and ¼ cup finely chopped walnuts.

Oysters Romano

**12 oysters, shucked and on the half shell
2 slices bacon, cut into 12 (1-inch) pieces
½ cup Italian-seasoned dry bread crumbs
2 tablespoons butter, melted
½ teaspoon garlic salt
6 tablespoons grated Romano, Parmesan or provolone cheese
Fresh chives (optional)**

1. Preheat oven to 375°F. Place shells with oysters on baking sheet. Top each oyster with 1 piece bacon. Bake 10 minutes or until bacon is crisp.

2. Meanwhile, combine bread crumbs, butter and garlic salt in small bowl. Spoon mixture over oysters; top with cheese. Bake 5 to 10 minutes or until cheese melts. Garnish with chives.   *Makes 12 appetizers*

The Famous Lipton® California Dip

Chicken Empanadas

1 box (15 ounces) refrigerated pie crusts (two 11-inch rounds)
4 ounces cream cheese
2 tablespoons chopped fresh cilantro
2 tablespoons salsa
½ teaspoon ground cumin
½ teaspoon salt
¼ teaspoon garlic powder
1 cup finely chopped cooked chicken
1 egg, beaten
Additional salsa

1. Remove pie crust pouches from box; let stand at room temperature 15 to 20 minutes.

2. Heat cream cheese in small heavy saucepan over low heat; cook and stir until melted. Add cilantro, salsa, cumin, salt and garlic powder; stir until smooth. Stir in chicken; remove from heat.

3. Preheat oven to 425°F. Line 2 baking sheets with foil. Unfold pie crusts; remove plastic film. Roll out slightly on lightly floured surface. Cut crusts into 3-inch rounds using biscuit cutter. Reroll pie crust scraps and cut enough additional to equal 20 rounds.

4. Place about 2 teaspoons chicken mixture in center of each round. Brush edges lightly with water. Pull one side of dough over filling to form half circle; pinch edges to seal.

5. Place 10 empanadas on each prepared baking sheet; brush lightly with egg. Bake 16 to 18 minutes or until lightly browned. Serve with salsa.

Makes 20 empanadas

Note: Empanadas can be prepared ahead of time and frozen. Simply wrap unbaked empanadas in plastic wrap and freeze. To bake, unwrap and follow directions in step 5, baking 18 to 20 minutes.

Chicken Empanadas

Classic Guacamole

4 tablespoons finely chopped white onion, divided
1 or 2 fresh serrano or jalapeño peppers,* seeded and finely chopped
1 tablespoon plus 1½ teaspoons coarsely chopped fresh cilantro, divided
¼ teaspoon chopped garlic
2 large soft avocados
1 medium tomato, peeled and chopped
1 to 2 teaspoons fresh lime juice
¼ teaspoon salt
Tortilla chips

*Serrano and jalapeño peppers can sting and irritate the skin; wear rubber gloves when handling peppers and do not touch eyes. Wash hands after handling.

1. Combine 2 tablespoons onion, peppers, 1 tablespoon cilantro and garlic in large mortar. Grind with pestle until almost smooth. (Mixture can be processed in blender, if necessary, but it may become more watery than desired.)

2. Cut avocados lengthwise into halves; remove and discard pits. Scoop out avocado flesh; place in bowl. Add pepper mixture. Mash roughly, leaving avocado slightly chunky.

3. Add tomato, lime juice, salt and remaining 2 tablespoons onion and 1½ teaspoons cilantro to avocado mixture; mix well. Serve immediately or cover and refrigerate up to 4 hours. Serve with tortilla chips. Garnish, if desired.

Makes about 2 cups

Classic Guacamole

Devilish Crab Puffs

Swiss Puffs (recipe on facing page)
2 cups crabmeat
¼ cup chopped fresh parsley
¼ cup mayonnaise
2 tablespoons finely minced onion
2 teaspoons white wine
1 teaspoon Worcestershire sauce
1 teaspoon dry mustard
1 teaspoon lemon juice
¼ teaspoon white pepper

1. Prepare Swiss Puffs; set aside.

2. To make filling, pick out and discard any shell or cartilage from crabmeat. Place crabmeat, parsley, mayonnaise, onion, wine, Worcestershire sauce, mustard, lemon juice and pepper in medium bowl. Stir gently to blend.

3. Preheat oven to 375°F. Fill Swiss Puffs with crab filling.

4. Place filled puffs on ungreased baking sheet; bake 10 minutes or until heated through. *Makes about 40 appetizers*

Swiss Puffs

½ cup milk
½ cup water
¼ cup (½ stick) butter
¼ teaspoon salt
   Pinch ground nutmeg
   Pinch white pepper
1 cup all-purpose flour
4 eggs, at room temperature
1 cup shredded Swiss cheese, divided

1. Preheat oven to 400°F. Grease 2 large baking sheets.

2. Heat milk, water, butter, salt, nutmeg and pepper in 3-quart saucepan over medium-high heat until mixture boils. Remove pan from heat; add flour all at once, mixing until smooth. Cook over medium-low heat, stirring constantly, until mixture leaves side of pan clean and forms a ball. Remove pan from heat.

3. Add eggs, 1 at a time, beating until smooth and shiny after each addition. Continue beating until mixture loses its gloss. Stir in ¾ cup cheese.

4. Drop rounded teaspoonfuls of batter 1 inch apart onto prepared baking sheets. Sprinkle with remaining ¼ cup cheese.

5. Bake 30 to 35 minutes or until puffs are golden brown. Cool completely on wire racks.

6. Before filling, cut tops off puffs; scoop out and discard moist dough in centers.

Makes about 40 puffs

Elegant Pork Terrine

2 tablespoons butter or margarine
1 cup chopped onion
2 cloves garlic, minced
1 pound sweet Italian sausage
1 pound ground pork
2 eggs, slightly beaten
¼ cup light cream
2 tablespoons brandy
⅛ teaspoon ground allspice
⅛ teaspoon ground cloves
⅛ teaspoon black pepper
½ pound Canadian bacon, cut into 4×½-inch strips
8 fresh asparagus spears

In large skillet melt butter. Add onion and garlic; cook and stir until tender. Remove from skillet and set aside.

Remove sausage from casing and crumble into skillet. Add ground pork and cook 4 minutes or until partially cooked. Drain pan drippings. Let pork mixture stand about 10 minutes to cool. Stir in onion mixture, eggs, light cream, brandy, allspice, cloves and pepper; mix well.

Spread ⅓ of meat mixture in lightly greased 8×4×2-inch loaf pan. Place Canadian bacon over meat mixture, making 3 rows. Top with ⅓ of meat mixture. Remove tough ends of asparagus. Arrange asparagus over meat mixture, making 4 rows. Top with remaining ⅓ of meat mixture.

Wrap entire loaf pan with heavy-duty foil, sealing edges. Fill large roasting pan about half full of water. Place loaf pan in roasting pan. Bake at 350°F 1 to 1½ hours or until done. Remove loaf pan from roasting pan; let stand about 15 minutes. Place another loaf pan filled with dried beans on top of terrine. Let stand 2 hours. Remove weight and refrigerate terrine overnight.

To serve, remove foil and loosen edges of terrine with knife. Turn out onto serving platter. Serve with assorted crackers. *Makes 16 servings*

Prep Time: 30 minutes
Cook Time: 90 minutes

*Favorite recipe from **National Pork Board***

Elegant Pork Terrine

Southern Crab Cakes with Rémoulade Dipping Sauce

10 ounces fresh lump crabmeat
1½ cups fresh white or sourdough bread crumbs, divided
¼ cup chopped green onions
½ cup mayonnaise, divided
1 egg white, lightly beaten
2 tablespoons coarse grain or spicy brown mustard, divided
¾ teaspoon hot pepper sauce, divided
2 teaspoons olive oil, divided
Lemon wedges

1. Preheat oven to 200°F. Pick out and discard any shell or cartilage from crabmeat. Combine crabmeat, ¾ cup bread crumbs and green onions in medium bowl. Add ¼ cup mayonnaise, egg white, 1 tablespoon mustard and ½ teaspoon pepper sauce; mix well. Using ¼ cup mixture per cake, shape into 8 (½-inch-thick) cakes. Roll crab cakes lightly in remaining ¾ cup bread crumbs.

2. Heat large nonstick skillet over medium heat; add 1 teaspoon oil. Add 4 crab cakes; cook 4 to 5 minutes per side or until golden brown. Transfer to serving platter; keep warm in oven. Repeat with remaining 1 teaspoon oil and crab cakes.

3. To prepare dipping sauce, combine remaining ¼ cup mayonnaise, 1 tablespoon mustard and ¼ teaspoon hot pepper sauce in small bowl; mix well.

4. Serve crab cakes warm with lemon wedges and dipping sauce.

Makes 8 crab cakes

Southern Crab Cakes with Rémoulade Dipping Sauce

Angelic Deviled Eggs

6 eggs
¼ cup cottage cheese
3 tablespoons prepared ranch dressing
2 teaspoons Dijon mustard
2 tablespoons minced fresh chives or dill
1 tablespoon diced well-drained pimiento or roasted red pepper

1. Place eggs in medium saucepan; add enough water to cover. Bring to a boil over medium heat. Remove from heat; cover. Let stand 15 minutes. Drain. Add cold water to eggs in saucepan; let stand until eggs are cool. Drain and peel.

2. Slice eggs lengthwise in half. Remove yolks, reserving 3 yolk halves. Discard remaining yolks or reserve for another use. Place egg whites, cut sides up, on serving plate; cover with plastic wrap. Refrigerate while preparing filling.

3. Combine cottage cheese, dressing, mustard and reserved yolk halves in food processor; process until smooth. (Or, place in small bowl and mash with fork until well blended.) Transfer mixture to small bowl; stir in chives and pimiento. Spoon into egg whites. Cover and chill at least 1 hour. *Makes 12 servings*

Angelic Deviled Eggs

Olive Tapenade Dip

1½ cups (10-ounce jar) pitted kalamata olives
3 tablespoons olive oil
3 tablespoons *French's*® **Bold n' Spicy Brown Mustard**
1 tablespoon minced fresh rosemary leaves *or* **1 teaspoon dried**
    rosemary leaves
1 teaspoon minced garlic

1. Place all ingredients in food processor. Process until puréed.

2. Serve with vegetable crudités or pita chips. *Makes 4 (¼-cup) servings*

Tip: To pit olives, place in plastic bag. Gently tap with wooden mallet or rolling pin until olives split open. Remove pits.

Prep Time: 10 minutes

tip

To make pita chips, preheat oven to 375°F. Split open each pita bread and separate sides into two circles. Arrange on baking sheet, rough side up. Bake 10 to 20 minutes until browned and crisp. When pita is cool, break into chip-size pieces. Store in air-tight container at room temperature.

Olive Tapenade Dip

Cheese Straws

½ cup (1 stick) butter, softened
⅛ teaspoon salt
  Dash ground red pepper
1 pound sharp Cheddar cheese, shredded, at room temperature
2 cups self-rising flour

Heat oven to 350°F. In mixer bowl, beat butter, salt and pepper until creamy. Add cheese; mix well. Gradually add flour, mixing until dough begins to form a ball. Form dough into ball with hands. Fit cookie press with small star plate; fill with dough according to manufacturer's directions. Press dough onto cookie sheets in 3-inch-long strips (or desired shapes). Bake 12 minutes or just until lightly browned. Cool completely on wire rack. Store tightly covered. *Makes about 10 dozen*

Favorite recipe from **Southeast United Dairy Industry Association, Inc.**

Classic Salsa

4 medium tomatoes
1 small onion, finely chopped
2 to 3 jalapeño peppers or serrano peppers,* seeded and minced
¼ cup chopped fresh cilantro
1 small clove garlic, minced
2 tablespoons lime juice
  Salt and black pepper

*Jalapeño and serrano peppers can sting and irritate the skin; wear rubber gloves when handling peppers and do not touch eyes. Wash hands after handling.

Cut tomatoes in half; remove seeds. Coarsely chop tomatoes. Combine tomatoes, onion, jalapeño peppers, cilantro, garlic and lime juice in medium bowl. Add salt and black pepper to taste. Cover and refrigerate 1 hour or up to 3 days for flavors to blend. *Makes about 2½ cups salsa*

Cheese Straws

Original Buffalo Chicken Wings

Zesty Blue Cheese Dip (recipe follows)
2½ pounds chicken wings, split and tips discarded
½ cup *Frank's® RedHot®* Original Cayenne Pepper Sauce (or to taste)
⅓ cup butter or margarine, melted
Celery sticks

1. Prepare Zesty Blue Cheese Dip.

2. Deep fry* wings at 400°F 12 minutes or until crisp and cooked through; drain.

3. Combine **Frank's RedHot** Sauce and butter in large bowl. Add wings to sauce; toss to coat evenly. Serve with Zesty Blue Cheese Dip and celery.

Makes 24 to 30 individual pieces

Or, prepare wings using one of the cooking methods below. Add wings to sauce; toss well to coat completely.

To Bake: Place wings in a single layer on rack in foil-lined roasting pan. Bake at 425°F 1 hour or until crisp and cooked through, turning halfway through baking time.

To Broil: Place wings in a single layer on rack in foil-lined roasting pan. Broil 6 inches from heat 15 to 20 minutes or until crisp and cooked through, turning once.

To Grill: Place wings on an oiled grid. Grill, over medium heat, 30 to 40 minutes or until crisp and cooked through, turning often.

Prep Time: 10 minutes
Cook Time: 15 minutes

Zesty Blue Cheese Dip

½ cup blue cheese salad dressing
¼ cup sour cream
2 teaspoons *Frank's® RedHot®* Original Cayenne Pepper Sauce

Combine all ingredients in medium serving bowl; mix well. Garnish with crumbled blue cheese, if desired.

Makes ¾ cup dip

Shanghai Red Wings: Cook chicken wings as directed on page 72. Combine ¼ cup soy sauce, 3 tablespoons honey, 3 tablespoons **Frank's RedHot** Sauce, 2 tablespoons peanut oil, 1 teaspoon grated peeled fresh ginger and 1 teaspoon minced garlic in small bowl. Mix well. Pour sauce over wings; toss well to coat evenly.

Cajun Wings: Cook chicken wings as directed on page 72. Combine ⅓ cup **Frank's RedHot** Sauce, ⅓ cup ketchup, ¼ cup (½ stick) melted butter or margarine and 2 teaspoons Cajun seasoning in small bowl. Mix well. Pour sauce over wings; toss well to coat evenly.

Santa Fe Wings: Cook chicken wings as directed on page 72. Combine ¼ cup (½ stick) melted butter or margarine, ¼ cup **Frank's RedHot** Sauce, ¼ cup chili sauce and 1 teaspoon chili powder in small bowl. Mix well. Pour sauce over wings; toss well to coat evenly.

Sweet 'n Spicy Wings: Cook chicken wings as directed on page 72. Combine ⅓ cup **Frank's RedHot** Sauce, ¼ cup (½ stick) butter, 2 tablespoons each thawed frozen orange juice concentrate and honey and ¼ teaspoon each ground cinnamon and ground allspice in small microwavable bowl. Microwave on HIGH 1 minute or until butter is melted. Stir until smooth. Pour sauce over wings; toss well to coat evenly.

Kentucky Style Wings: Cook chicken wings as directed on page 72. Combine ¼ cup (½ stick) melted butter or margarine, ¼ cup **Frank's RedHot** Sauce, 2 tablespoons pancake syrup and 2 tablespoons bourbon in large bowl. Mix well. Pour sauce over wings; toss well to coat evenly.

Prep Time: 5 minutes

Clams Casino

8 slices bacon, chopped
1 medium onion, chopped
1 green bell pepper, chopped
1 red bell pepper, chopped
1 cup (2 sticks) butter, softened
¼ cup lemon juice
⅛ teaspoon ground red pepper
2 dozen medium cherrystone clams, scrubbed, shucked and
chopped; 3 tablespoons clam juice reserved
¼ cup Italian-style bread crumbs

1. Cook and stir bacon in large skillet over medium-high heat until crisp. Remove with slotted spoon; drain on paper towels. Set bacon aside.

2. Preheat oven to 350°F. Discard all but 1 tablespoon bacon drippings from skillet. Cook and stir onion and bell peppers in same skillet over medium-high heat until onion is tender but not brown. Let stand at room temperature to cool slightly.

3. Combine butter and lemon juice in small bowl; mix well. Add bacon, onion mixture and ground red pepper.

4. In another small bowl, combine clams, reserved clam juice and bread crumbs.

5. Place clam shells on baking sheets. Fill clam shells half full with clam mixture and top with 1 tablespoon butter mixture.*

6. Bake 20 minutes or until lightly browned. Garnish as desired.

Makes about 16 appetizers

Clams may be frozen at this point. When ready to serve, place frozen clams on baking sheet; bake in a preheated 350°F oven 20 to 25 minutes.

Clams Casino

Crab Canapés

⅔ cup cream cheese, softened
2 teaspoons lemon juice
1 teaspoon hot pepper sauce
1 package (8 ounces) imitation crabmeat or lobster, flaked
⅓ cup chopped red bell pepper
2 green onions with tops, sliced (about ¼ cup)
64 cucumber slices (about 2½ medium cucumbers cut into ⅜-inch-thick slices) or melba toast rounds
Fresh parsley (optional)

1. Combine cream cheese, lemon juice and hot pepper sauce in medium bowl; mix well. Stir in crabmeat, bell pepper and green onions; cover. Chill at least 1 hour to allow flavors to blend.

2. When ready to serve, spoon 1½ teaspoons crabmeat mixture onto each cucumber slice. Place on serving plate; garnish with parsley, if desired.

Makes 64 canapés

tip

Imitation seafood (sometimes called "surimi") comes in different forms and flavors, including imitation crabmeat flakes and imitation lobster chunks. It is an economical way to enjoy the flavor of the real thing. Imitation seafood will keep unopened for 2 months. Once opened it should be used within 3 days.

Crab Canapés

Fried Calamari with Tartar Sauce

1 pound cleaned squid (body tubes, tentacles or a combination)
1 egg
1 tablespoon milk
¾ cup fine dry unseasoned bread crumbs
   Vegetable oil
   Tartar sauce
   Lemon wedges (optional)

1. Rinse squid under cold running water.

2. Cut each squid body crosswise into ¼-inch rings. Pat pieces thoroughly dry with paper towels.

3. Beat egg with milk in small bowl. Add squid pieces; stir to coat well. Spread bread crumbs on plate. Dip squid pieces in bread crumbs; place in shallow bowl or on waxed paper. Let stand 10 to 15 minutes before frying.

4. To deep fry squid, heat 1½ inches oil in large saucepan to 350°F. (Caution: Squid will pop and spatter during frying; do not stand too close to pan.) Adjust heat to maintain temperature. Fry 8 to 10 pieces of squid at a time in hot oil 45 to 60 seconds until light brown. Remove with slotted spoon; drain on paper towels. Repeat with remaining squid pieces. Do not overcook squid or it will become tough.

5. Serve hot with tartar sauce and lemon wedges. Garnish as desired.

Makes 4 servings

Variation: To shallow fry squid, heat about ¼ inch oil in large skillet over medium-high heat; reduce heat to medium. Add as many pieces of squid that fit in a single layer without crowding to hot oil. Cook, turning once, 1 minute per side or until light brown. Proceed as directed in step 5.

Fried Calamari with Tartar Sauce

Spinach Feta Triangles

¼ cup olive oil
½ cup chopped onion
2 eggs
**3 packages (10 ounces each) frozen chopped spinach, thawed and
    well drained**
16 ounces feta cheese, drained and crumbled
½ cup minced fresh parsley
**2 tablespoons chopped fresh oregano *or* 1 teaspoon dried oregano
    Salt and black pepper**
**1 package (16 ounces) frozen phyllo dough, thawed to room
    temperature**
1 cup (2 sticks) butter, melted

1. Preheat oven to 375°F. Heat oil over medium-high heat in small skillet. Add onion; cook and stir until translucent and golden.

2. Beat eggs in large bowl with electric mixer on medium-high speed until light and lemon colored. Add onion mixture, spinach, feta cheese, parsley and oregano; stir until blended. Season with salt and pepper.

3. Remove phyllo from package; unroll and place on large sheet of waxed paper. Fold phyllo crosswise into thirds. Use scissors to cut along folds into thirds. Cover phyllo with large sheet of plastic wrap and damp, clean kitchen towel.

4. Lay 1 strip of phyllo at a time on flat surface and brush immediately with melted butter. Fold strip in half lengthwise. Brush with butter again. Place rounded teaspoonful of spinach filling on 1 end of strip; fold over 1 corner to make triangle. Continue folding end to end, as you would fold a flag, keeping edges straight. Brush top with butter. Repeat process until all filling is used up.

5. Place triangles in single layer, seam side down, on ungreased baking sheet. Bake 20 minutes or until lightly browned. Serve warm.   *Makes 5 dozen appetizers*

Spinach Feta Triangles

Finger Food

Bite Size Tacos

1 pound ground beef
1 package (1.25 ounces) taco seasoning mix
2 cups *French's*® French Fried Onions
¼ cup chopped fresh cilantro
32 bite-size round tortilla chips
¾ cup sour cream
1 cup shredded Cheddar cheese

1. Cook beef in nonstick skillet over medium-high heat 5 minutes or until browned; drain. Stir in taco seasoning mix, *¾ cup water, 1 cup* French Fried Onions and cilantro. Simmer 5 minutes or until flavors are blended, stirring often.

2. Preheat oven to 350°F. Arrange tortilla chips on foil-lined baking sheet. Top with beef mixture, sour cream, remaining onions and cheese.

3. Bake 5 minutes or until cheese is melted and onions are golden.

Makes 8 appetizer servings

Prep Time: 5 minutes
Cook Time: 15 minutes

Bite Size Tacos

Pizza Breadsticks

1 package (¼ ounce) active dry yeast
¾ cup warm water (105° to 115°F)
2½ cups all-purpose flour
½ cup (2 ounces) shredded mozzarella cheese
¼ cup (1 ounce) shredded Parmesan cheese
¼ cup chopped red bell pepper
1 green onion with top, sliced
1 medium clove garlic, minced
½ teaspoon dried basil
½ teaspoon dried oregano
¼ teaspoon salt
¼ teaspoon red pepper flakes (optional)
1 tablespoon olive oil

1. Preheat oven to 400°F. Spray 2 large baking sheets with nonstick cooking spray; set aside.

2. Sprinkle yeast over warm water in small bowl; stir until yeast dissolves. Let stand 5 minutes or until bubbly.

3. Meanwhile, place all remaining ingredients except olive oil in food processor; process a few seconds to combine. With food processor running, gradually add yeast mixture and olive oil. Process just until mixture forms a ball. (Add an additional 2 tablespoons flour if dough is too sticky.)

4. Transfer dough to lightly floured surface; knead 1 minute. Let dough rest 5 minutes. Roll out dough with lightly floured rolling pin to form 14×8-inch rectangle; cut dough crosswise into ½-inch-wide strips. Twist dough strips; place on prepared baking sheets.

5. Bake 14 to 16 minutes or until lightly browned. *Makes 14 breadsticks*

Pizza Breadsticks

Skewered Antipasto

1 jar (8 ounces) SONOMA® marinated dried tomatoes
1 pound (3 medium) new potatoes, cooked until tender
2 cups bite-sized vegetable pieces (such as celery, bell peppers, radishes, carrots, cucumber and green onions)
1 cup drained cooked egg tortellini and/or spinach tortellini
1 tablespoon chopped fresh chives *or* 1 teaspoon dried chives
1 tablespoon chopped fresh rosemary *or* 1 teaspoon dried rosemary

Drain oil from tomatoes into medium bowl. Place tomatoes in small bowl; set aside. Cut potatoes into 1-inch cubes. Add potatoes, vegetables, tortellini, chives and rosemary to oil in medium bowl. Stir to coat with oil; cover and marinate 1 hour at room temperature. To assemble, alternately thread tomatoes, potatoes, vegetables and tortellini onto 6-inch skewers. *Makes 12 to 14 skewers*

Mini Tuna Tarts

1 (3-ounce) STARKIST Flavor Fresh Pouch® Tuna (Albacore or Chunk Light)
2 tablespoons mayonnaise
2 tablespoons sweet pickle relish
1 green onion, including top, minced
¾ cup shredded Monterey Jack cheese
Salt and pepper to taste
1 package (10 count) refrigerated flaky biscuits

Combine tuna, mayonnaise, pickle relish, onion and cheese; mix well. Add salt and pepper. Separate each biscuit into 2 halves. Press each half in bottom of lightly greased muffin pan to form a cup. Spoon scant tablespoon tuna mixture into each muffin cup. Bake in preheated 400°F oven 8 to 10 minutes or until edges of biscuits are just golden. Serve hot or cold. *Makes 20 servings*

Prep Time: 15 minutes

Skewered Antipasto

Quick Sausage Appetizers

½ pound BOB EVANS® Italian Roll Sausage
⅓ cup mozzarella cheese
¼ cup sour cream
3 tablespoons mayonnaise
2 tablespoons chopped green onion
½ teaspoon Worcestershire sauce
10 slices white bread*

*Party rye or thinly sliced French bread can be used instead of white bread. Double recipe to have enough sausage mixture.

Preheat broiler. Crumble and cook sausage in medium skillet until browned. Drain on paper towels. Transfer sausage to small bowl; stir in cheese, sour cream, mayonnaise, green onion and Worcestershire. Cut crusts from bread. Cut each slice into 4 squares; spread about 1 teaspoon sausage mixture onto each square. Arrange squares on ungreased baking sheet; place under hot broiler just until cheese melts and topping bubbles. (Be careful not to burn corners and edges.) Serve hot.

Makes 40 appetizer squares

Note: Quick Sausage Appetizers may be made ahead and refrigerated overnight or frozen up to 1 month before broiling.

tip

Like many recipes for canapés, this one calls for removing the crusts from the bread. To make use of reserved crusts, turn them into bread crumbs. Place them in a food processor and pulse until coarse crumbs form. Store the homemade bread crumbs in a resealable food storage bag in the freezer. Use them to bread chicken or fish, to sprinkle over casseroles, or in meat loaf or burgers.

Quick Sausage Appetizers

Taco Chicken Nachos

2 boneless skinless chicken breasts (about 8 ounces)
1 tablespoon plus 1½ teaspoons taco seasoning mix
1 teaspoon olive oil
¾ cup sour cream
1 can (4 ounces) chopped mild green chilies, drained
¼ cup minced red onion
1 bag (8 ounces) tortilla chips
1 cup (4 ounces) shredded Cheddar or Monterey Jack cheese
½ cup chopped fresh tomato
¼ cup pitted ripe olive slices (optional)
2 tablespoons chopped fresh cilantro (optional)

1. Bring 2 cups water to a boil in small saucepan. Add chicken. Reduce heat to low; cover. Simmer 10 minutes or until chicken is no longer pink in center. Remove from saucepan; cool. Chop chicken.

2. Combine taco seasoning mix and oil in small bowl; mix until smooth paste forms. Stir in sour cream. Add chicken, green chilies and onion; mix lightly.

3. Preheat broiler. Arrange tortilla chips on small ovenproof plates or large platter. Cover chips with chicken mixture and cheese. Broil 4 inches from heat 2 to 3 minutes or until chicken mixture is hot and cheese is melted. Sprinkle evenly with tomato, olives and cilantro, if desired. Serve hot. *Makes 12 servings*

Taco Chicken Nachos

Herbed Potato Chips

> **Nonstick olive oil cooking spray**
> **2 medium red potatoes (about ½ pound), unpeeled**
> **1 tablespoon olive oil**
> **2 tablespoons minced fresh dill, thyme or rosemary *or* 2 teaspoons dried dill weed, thyme or rosemary**
> **¼ teaspoon garlic salt**
> **⅛ teaspoon black pepper**
> **1¼ cups sour cream**

1. Preheat oven to 450°F. Spray large baking sheets with cooking spray; set aside.

2. Cut potatoes crosswise into very thin slices, about ¹⁄₁₆ inch thick. Pat dry with paper towels. Arrange potato slices in single layer on prepared baking sheets; coat potatoes with cooking spray.

3. Bake 10 minutes; turn slices over. Brush with oil. Combine dill, garlic salt and pepper in small bowl; sprinkle evenly onto potato slices. Continue baking 5 to 10 minutes or until potatoes are golden brown. Cool on baking sheets.

4. Serve with sour cream.

Makes 6 servings

Deviled Mixed Nuts

> **3 tablespoons vegetable oil**
> **2 cups assorted unsalted nuts**
> **2 tablespoons sugar**
> **1 teaspoon paprika**
> **½ teaspoon chili powder**
> **½ teaspoon curry powder**
> **½ teaspoon ground cumin**
> **½ teaspoon ground coriander**
> **½ teaspoon black pepper**
> **¼ teaspoon salt**

Heat oil in large skillet over medium heat; cook and stir nuts in hot oil 2 to 3 minutes or until browned. Combine remaining ingredients in small bowl; sprinkle over nuts. Stir to coat evenly. Heat 1 to 2 minutes more. Drain nuts on paper towels.

Makes 2 cups

Herbed Potato Chips

Mexican Shrimp Cocktail

½ cup WISH-BONE® Italian Dressing*
½ cup chopped tomato
1 can (4 ounces) chopped green chilies, undrained
¼ cup chopped green onions
1½ teaspoons honey
¼ teaspoon hot pepper sauce
1 pound medium shrimp, cleaned and cooked
2 teaspoons finely chopped cilantro or parsley

Also terrific with WISH-BONE® Robusto Italian or Just 2 Good! Italian Dressing.

In medium bowl, combine Italian dressing, tomato, chilies, green onions, honey and hot pepper sauce. Stir in shrimp. Cover and marinate in refrigerator, stirring occasionally, at least 2 hours. Just before serving, stir in cilantro.

Makes about 6 servings

Cheddar Tomato Bacon Toasts

1 jar (1 pound) RAGÚ® Cheesy!® Double Cheddar Sauce
1 medium tomato, chopped
5 slices bacon, crisp-cooked and crumbled (about ⅓ cup)
2 loaves Italian bread (each about 16 inches long), each cut into 16 slices

1. Preheat oven to 350°F. In medium bowl, combine Ragú Cheesy! Sauce, tomato and bacon.

2. On baking sheet, arrange bread slices. Evenly top with sauce mixture.

3. Bake 10 minutes or until sauce mixture is bubbling. Serve immediately.

Makes 32 toasts

Prep Time: 10 minutes
Cook Time: 10 minutes

Mexican Shrimp Cocktail

Mini Crab Cakes

1 pound crabmeat
1 cup fine, dry bread crumbs, divided
2 eggs, beaten
¼ cup minced onion
¼ cup minced green bell pepper
¼ cup minced red bell pepper
1 teaspoon dry mustard
½ teaspoon TABASCO® brand Pepper Sauce
Salt to taste
Vegetable oil
Zesty Rémoulade Sauce (recipe follows)
Fresh dill (optional)

Combine crabmeat, ½ cup bread crumbs, eggs, onion, bell peppers, mustard, TABASCO® Sauce and salt in large bowl. Cover and refrigerate 1 to 2 hours or until mixture becomes firm. Shape mixture into small cakes, about 1½×1 inches. Coat cakes in remaining ½ cup bread crumbs.

Pour oil into heavy skillet to depth of ⅓ inch; heat skillet over medium heat. When oil is hot, cook crab cakes about 3 to 5 minutes on each side or until browned. Remove to paper towels. Serve crab cakes warm; top with dollops of Zesty Rémoulade Sauce. Garnish with dill sprigs, if desired. *Makes 20 to 25 cakes*

Zesty Rémoulade Sauce

1 cup mayonnaise
2 to 3 green onions, finely chopped
1 rib celery, finely chopped
2 tablespoons prepared horseradish, drained
1 tablespoon finely chopped chives
1 tablespoon Dijon mustard
1 tablespoon fresh lemon juice
1 clove garlic, finely chopped
½ teaspoon TABASCO® brand Pepper Sauce

Combine all ingredients in medium bowl. Cover and refrigerate 1 hour to blend flavors. Serve chilled. *Makes 1¾ cups*

Mini Crab Cakes with Zesty Rémoulade Sauce

Devilish Eggs

12 hard-cooked eggs, cut in half
6 tablespoons low-fat mayonnaise
2 tablespoons _French's_® Classic Yellow® Mustard
¼ teaspoon salt
⅛ teaspoon ground red pepper

1. Remove yolk from egg whites using teaspoon. Press yolks through sieve with back of spoon or mash with fork in medium bowl. Stir in mayonnaise, mustard, salt and pepper; mix well.

2. Spoon or pipe yolk mixture into egg whites. Arrange on serving platter. Garnish as desired. Cover; chill in refrigerator until ready to serve.   *Makes 12 servings*

Zesty Variations: Stir in one of the following: 2 tablespoons minced red onion plus 1 tablespoon horseradish, 2 tablespoons pickle relish plus 1 tablespoon minced fresh dill, 2 tablespoons each minced onion and celery plus 1 tablespoon minced fresh dill, ¼ cup (1 ounce) shredded Cheddar cheese plus ½ teaspoon **French's**® Worcestershire Sauce.

Tomato and Caper Crostini

1 French roll, cut into 8 slices
2 plum tomatoes, finely chopped (about 4 ounces)
1½ tablespoons capers
1½ teaspoons dried basil
1 teaspoon extra-virgin olive oil
1 ounce crumbled feta with sun-dried tomatoes and basil or any variety

1. Preheat oven to 350°F.

2. Place bread slices on ungreased baking sheet in single layer. Bake 15 minutes or just until golden brown. Cool completely.

3. Meanwhile, combine tomatoes, capers, basil and oil in small bowl.

4. Just before serving, spoon tomato mixture on each bread slice; sprinkle with cheese.
                                                                  Makes 8 crostini

Devilish Eggs

Zucchini Pizza Bites

⅓ cup salsa
¼ pound chorizo sausage*
2 small zucchini, trimmed and cut diagonally into ¼-inch thick slices
6 tablespoons shredded mozzarella cheese

*If chorizo is unavailable, substitute any variety of spicy sausage.

1. Preheat oven to 400°F. Place salsa in fine sieve and press out excess moisture; set aside to drain.

2. Remove sausage from casing. Brown sausage in small skillet over medium-high heat, stirring to break up meat; drain.

3. Place zucchini on baking sheet. Spoon 1 teaspoon drained salsa on each zucchini slice. Top with chorizo, dividing evenly among zucchini slices. Sprinkle 1½ teaspoons cheese over each slice.

4. Bake 10 minutes or until cheese melts. *Makes 6 servings*

tip

Chorizo is a spicy pork sausage common to both Mexican and Spanish cuisine. The Mexican variety (which is the kind most widely available in the United States) is made from raw pork. The Spanish variety is traditionally made from smoked pork. Most Mexican chorizo sold in the supermarket comes in a plastic casing which must be removed before cooking.

Zucchini Pizza Bites

Fast Pesto Focaccia

1 can (10 ounces) refrigerated pizza crust dough
2 tablespoons prepared pesto
4 sun-dried tomatoes (packed in oil), drained

1. Preheat oven to 425°F. Lightly grease 8-inch square pan. Unroll pizza dough. Fold in half; pat into pan.

2. Spread pesto evenly over dough. Chop tomatoes or snip with kitchen scissors; sprinkle over pesto. Press tomatoes into dough. Using wooden spoon handle, make indentations in dough every 2 inches.

3. Bake 10 to 12 minutes or until golden brown. Cut into 16 squares and serve warm or at room temperature. *Makes 16 squares*

Prep and Cook Time: 20 minutes

Pinwheel Ham Bites

2 packages (6½ ounces each) garlic-and-herb spreadable cheese, softened
4 (¹⁄₁₆-inch-thick) slices boiled ham
40 round buttery crackers

1. Spread ½ package cheese to edges of each ham slice. Beginning at short end, roll up tightly. Wrap tightly in plastic wrap; refrigerate rolls at least 2 hours.

2. Cut each roll crosswise into 10 slices. Place 1 slice on each cracker. Serve immediately. *Makes 40 appetizers*

Prep Time: 30 minutes
Chill Time: 2 hours

Fast Pesto Focaccia

Triangle Tostadas

2 large (burrito size) flour tortillas
Vegetable oil
1 package (about 1 pound) lean ground pork
1 package (1 ounce) LAWRY'S® Taco Spices & Seasonings
⅔ cup water
1 can (16 ounces) refried beans, warmed

Toppings
Shredded lettuce and cheese, chopped tomatoes

Preheat oven to 400°F. Cut each tortilla into quarters, forming 4 triangles. Place triangles in single layer on baking sheet. Brush each side of triangle lightly with oil. Bake for 4 to 5 minutes or until golden brown and crispy; let cool. Meanwhile, in large skillet, brown ground pork over medium high heat until crumbly, drain fat. Stir in Taco Spices & Seasonings and water. Bring to a boil; reduce heat to low and cook, uncovered for 7 minutes or until pork is thoroughly cooked, stirring occasionally. To assemble tostadas, evenly divide and spread refried beans on each tortilla triangle. Spread about ¼ cup seasoned pork on top of beans. Top with shredded lettuce, cheese and tomatoes, as desired. *Makes 8 tostadas*

Variations: Cut each tortilla into 8 pieces and make mini appetizer tostadas. For additional toppings try sliced black olives, sour cream, guacamole, salsa or jalapeño peppers.

Prep Time: 15 minutes
Cook Time: 16 to 18 minutes

Triangle Tostada

Savory Pita Chips

2 whole wheat or white rounds pita bread
Nonstick olive oil cooking spray
3 tablespoons grated Parmesan cheese
1 teaspoon dried basil leaves
¼ teaspoon garlic powder

1. Preheat oven to 350°F. Line baking sheet with foil; set aside.

2. Using scissors, carefully cut each pita bread around edges to form 2 rounds. Cut each round into 6 wedges.

3. Place wedges, rough side down, on prepared baking sheet; coat lightly with cooking spray. Turn wedges over; spray again.

4. Combine Parmesan cheese, basil and garlic powder in small bowl; sprinkle evenly over pita wedges.

5. Bake 12 to 14 minutes or until golden brown. Cool completely.

Makes 12 chips

Cinnamon Crisps: Substitute butter-flavored cooking spray for olive oil cooking spray, and 1 tablespoon sugar mixed with ¼ teaspoon ground cinnamon for Parmesan cheese, basil and garlic powder.

tip

Pita bread (sometimes called pocket bread) is a Middle Eastern flat bread that splits open horizontally to form a pocket. Wedges of pita are traditionally served with dips such as hummus or baba ganoush. Toasting pita creates savory chips, as in this recipe. You can also experiment with other seasonings, such as chili powder or Italian seasoning, on toasted pita chips.

Savory Pita Chips

Mini Chick-Pea Cakes

1 can (15 ounces) chick-peas, rinsed and drained
1 cup shredded carrots
⅓ cup seasoned dry bread crumbs
¼ cup creamy Italian salad dressing
1 egg

1. Preheat oven to 375°F. Spray baking sheet with nonstick cooking spray.

2. Mash chick-peas coarsely in medium bowl with hand potato masher. Stir in carrots, bread crumbs, salad dressing and egg; mix well.

3. Shape chick-pea mixture into small patties, using about 1 tablespoon mixture for each. Place on prepared baking sheet.

4. Bake 15 to 18 minutes, turning over halfway through baking time, until chick-pea cakes are lightly browned on both sides. Serve warm with additional salad dressing for dipping, if desired. *Makes about 2 dozen appetizers*

Summer Fruits with Peanut Butter-Honey Dip

⅓ cup smooth or chunky peanut butter
2 tablespoons milk
2 tablespoons honey
1 tablespoon apple juice or water
⅛ teaspoon ground cinnamon
2 cups melon balls, including cantaloupe and honeydew
1 peach or nectarine, pitted and cut into 8 wedges
1 banana, peeled and thickly sliced

1. Place peanut butter in small bowl; gradually stir in milk and honey until blended. Stir in apple juice and cinnamon until mixture is smooth.

2. Serve dip with fruit. *Makes 4 servings (about ½ cup dip)*

Prep Time: 20 minutes

Mini Chick-Pea Cakes

Home-Style Corn Cakes

    1 cup yellow cornmeal
    ½ cup all-purpose flour
    ½ teaspoon baking powder
    ½ teaspoon baking soda
    1 envelope LIPTON® RECIPE SECRETS® Onion Soup Mix*
    ¾ cup buttermilk
    1 egg, beaten
    1 can (17¼ ounces) cream-style corn
    2 ounces roasted red peppers, chopped (about ¼ cup)
       I CAN'T BELIEVE IT'S NOT BUTTER!® Spread

*Or, substitute Lipton® RECIPE SECRETS® Golden Onion Soup Mix.

In large bowl, combine cornmeal, flour, baking powder and baking soda. Blend soup mix with buttermilk, egg, corn and roasted red peppers; stir into cornmeal mixture.

In 12-inch nonstick skillet or on griddle, melt ½ teaspoon I Can't Believe It's Not Butter!® Spread over medium heat. Drop ¼ cup batter for each corn cake and cook, turning once, 5 minutes or until cooked through and golden brown. Remove to serving platter and keep warm. Repeat with remaining batter and additional I Can't Believe It's Not Butter!® Spread if needed. Serve with sour cream and prepared salsa, if desired.

Makes about 18 corn cakes

Tip: Leftover corn cakes may be wrapped and frozen. Remove from wrapping and reheat straight from freezer in preheated 350°F oven for 15 minutes.

Microwave Sweet Potato Chips

    2 cups thinly sliced sweet potatoes
    1 tablespoon packed brown sugar
    2 teaspoons margarine

Microwave Directions

Place sweet potatoes in single layer in microwavable dish. Sprinkle with water. Microwave at HIGH 5 minutes. Stir in brown sugar and margarine. Microwave at HIGH 2 to 3 minutes. Let stand a few minutes before serving.   *Makes 4 servings*

*Favorite recipe from **The Sugar Association, Inc.***

Home-Style Corn Cakes

Mini Pizzas

CRUST
 ⅓ cup olive oil
 1 tablespoon TABASCO® brand Pepper Sauce
 2 large cloves garlic, minced
 1 teaspoon dried rosemary, crumbled
 1 (16-ounce) package hot roll mix with yeast packet
1¼ cups hot water

GOAT CHEESE TOPPING
 1 large tomato, diced
 ¼ cup crumbled goat cheese
 2 tablespoons chopped fresh parsley

ROASTED PEPPER AND OLIVE TOPPING
 ½ cup shredded mozzarella cheese
 ½ cup pitted green olives
 ⅓ cup roasted red pepper strips

ARTICHOKE TOPPING
 ½ cup chopped artichoke hearts
 ½ cup cherry tomatoes, sliced into wedges
 ⅓ cup sliced green onions

For crust, combine olive oil, TABASCO® Sauce, garlic and rosemary in small bowl. Combine hot roll mix, yeast packet, hot water and 2 tablespoons oil mixture in large bowl; stir until dough pulls away from side of bowl. Turn dough onto lightly floured surface; shape into ball. Knead until smooth, adding additional flour as necessary.

Preheat oven to 425°F. For toppings, combine ingredients in separate bowls. Cut dough into quarters; cut each quarter into 10 equal pieces. Roll each piece into ball. Press each ball into 2-inch round on large cookie sheet; brush each round with remaining oil mixture. Arrange about 2 teaspoons topping on each dough round. Bake 12 minutes or until dough is lightly browned and puffed.

Makes 40 appetizers

Mini Pizzas

Mini Sausage Quiches

½ cup butter or margarine, softened
3 ounces cream cheese, softened
1 cup all-purpose flour
½ pound BOB EVANS® Italian Roll Sausage
1 cup (4 ounces) shredded Swiss cheese
1 tablespoon snipped fresh chives
2 eggs
1 cup half-and-half
¼ teaspoon salt
   Dash cayenne pepper

Beat butter and cream cheese in medium bowl until creamy. Blend in flour; refrigerate 1 hour. Roll into 24 (1-inch) balls; press each into ungreased mini-muffin cup to form pastry shell. Preheat oven to 375°F. To prepare filling, crumble sausage into small skillet. Cook over medium heat until browned, stirring occasionally. Drain off any drippings. Sprinkle evenly into pastry shells in muffin cups; sprinkle with Swiss cheese and chives. Whisk eggs, half-and-half, salt and cayenne until blended; pour into pastry shells. Bake 20 to 30 minutes or until set. Remove from pans. Serve hot. Refrigerate leftovers. *Makes 24 appetizers*

Tip: Pour mixture into 12 standard 2½-inch muffin cups to make larger individual quiches. Serve for breakfast.

Mini Sausage Quiches

Dips & Spreads

Smoky Eggplant Dip

1 large eggplant (about 1 pound)
¼ cup olive oil
3 tablespoons *Frank's®* RedHot® Original Cayenne Pepper Sauce
2 tablespoons peanut butter or tahini paste
1 tablespoon lemon juice
2 cloves garlic, minced
¾ teaspoon salt
½ teaspoon ground cumin
   Spicy Pita Chips (recipe follows)

1. Prepare grill. Place eggplant on oiled grid. Grill, over hot coals, 15 minutes or until soft and skin is charred, turning often. Remove from grill; cool until easy enough to handle.

2. Peel skin from eggplant with paring knife; discard. Coarsely chop eggplant. Place in strainer or kitchen towel. Press out excess liquid.

3. Place eggplant in food processor; add oil, **Frank's RedHot** Sauce, peanut butter, lemon juice, garlic, salt and cumin. Cover; process until mixture is very smooth. Transfer to serving bowl. Cover; refrigerate until chilled. Serve with Spicy Pita Chips.

Makes 1½ cups dip

Spicy Pita Chips: Split 4 pita bread rounds in half lengthwise. Combine ½ cup olive oil, ¼ cup **Frank's RedHot** Sauce and 1 tablespoon minced garlic in small bowl. Brush mixture on both sides of pitas. Place pitas on grid. Grill, over medium coals, about 5 minutes or until crispy, turning once. Cut pitas into triangles.

Prep Time: 30 minutes
Cook Time: 20 minutes
Chill Time: 30 minutes

Smoky Eggplant Dip

Rio Grande Salsa

1 tablespoon vegetable oil
1 onion, chopped
3 cloves garlic, minced
2 teaspoons ground cumin
1½ teaspoons chili powder
2 cans (14½ ounces each) diced tomatoes, drained
1 canned chipotle pepper in adobo sauce, minced
1 teaspoon adobo sauce from canned chipotle pepper
½ cup chopped fresh cilantro
¾ teaspoon sugar
½ teaspoon salt

1. Heat oil in medium saucepan over medium-high heat. Add onion and garlic. Cook and stir 5 minutes or until onion is tender. Add cumin and chili powder; cook 30 seconds, stirring frequently. Add tomatoes, chipotle pepper and adobo sauce. Reduce heat to medium-low. Simmer 10 to 12 minutes or until salsa is thickened, stirring occasionally.

2. Remove from heat; stir in cilantro, sugar and salt. Cool completely. Store in airtight container in refrigerator up to 3 weeks. *Makes about 3 cups salsa*

Note: This salsa is very spicy. For a milder version, use only 1 teaspoon finely diced chipotle chili pepper.

Rio Grande Salsa

Pizza Fondue

½ pound bulk Italian sausage
1 cup chopped onion
2 jars (26 ounces each) meatless pasta sauce
4 ounces thinly sliced ham, finely chopped
1 package (3 ounces) sliced pepperoni, finely chopped
¼ teaspoon red pepper flakes
1 pound mozzarella cheese, cut into ¾-inch cubes
1 loaf Italian or French bread, cut into 1-inch cubes

Slow Cooker Directions

1. Cook sausage and onion in large skillet until sausage is browned; drain fat.

2. Transfer sausage mixture to slow cooker. Stir in pasta sauce, ham, pepperoni and pepper flakes. Cover; cook on LOW 3 to 4 hours.

3. Serve fondue with cheese and bread cubes.

Makes 20 to 25 appetizer servings

Prep Time: 15 minutes
Cook Time: 3 to 4 hours

Zesty Fun Pretzel Dip

½ cup *French's®* Bold n' Spicy Brown Mustard
½ cup honey

1. Combine mustard and honey.

2. Use for dipping pretzels, chips or cheese cubes.

Makes 1 cup dip

Prep Time: 5 minutes

Pizza Fondue

7-Layer Ranch Dip

1 envelope LIPTON® RECIPE SECRETS® Ranch Soup Mix
1 container (16 ounces) sour cream
1 cup shredded lettuce
1 medium tomato, chopped (about 1 cup)
1 can (2.25 ounces) sliced pitted ripe olives, drained
¼ cup chopped red onion
1 can (4.5 ounces) chopped green chilies, drained
1 cup shredded Cheddar cheese (about 4 ounces)

1. In 2-quart shallow dish, combine soup mix and sour cream.

2. Evenly layer remaining ingredients, ending with cheese. Chill, if desired. Serve with tortilla chips.   *Makes 7 cups dip*

Prep Time: 15 minutes

Curried Fruit Dip

1 cup sour cream
3 tablespoons mango chutney
2 tablespoons unsweetened pineapple juice
2 teaspoons honey Dijon mustard
1 teaspoon curry powder
1 teaspoon grated orange peel
   Assorted cut-up fresh fruit and vegetables

1. Place sour cream in small bowl. Stir in chutney, pineapple juice, mustard, curry and orange peel until well blended.

2. Transfer dip to serving bowl. Serve immediately with fresh fruit and vegetables or cover with plastic wrap and refrigerate until ready to serve.   *Makes 1½ cups dip*

Note: Curry powder is a blend of up to 20 ground spices, herbs and seeds. It should be stored in an airtight container to preserve its pungency.

Prep Time: 10 minutes

7-Layer Ranch Dip

Nutty Carrot Spread

¼ cup finely chopped pecans
6 ounces cream cheese, softened
2 tablespoons frozen orange juice concentrate, thawed
¼ teaspoon ground cinnamon
1 cup shredded carrots
¼ cup raisins
36 party pumpernickel bread slices, toasted, or melba toast rounds

1. Preheat oven to 350°F. Place pecans in shallow baking pan. Bake 10 minutes or until lightly toasted, stirring occasionally.

2. Meanwhile, combine cream cheese, orange juice concentrate and cinnamon in small bowl; stir until well blended. Stir in carrots, pecans and raisins.

3. Serve spread with bread or crackers.   *Makes 18 servings*

Hot French Onion Dip

1 envelope LIPTON® RECIPE SECRETS® Onion Soup Mix
1 container (16 ounces) sour cream
2 cups shredded Swiss cheese (about 8 ounces), divided
¼ cup HELLMANN'S® or BEST FOODS® Real Mayonnaise

1. Preheat oven to 375°F. In 1-quart casserole, combine soup mix, sour cream, 1¾ cups Swiss cheese and mayonnaise.

2. Bake uncovered 20 minutes or until heated through. Sprinkle with remaining ¼ cup cheese.

3. Serve, if desired, with sliced French bread or your favorite dippers.

Makes 2 cups dip

Nutty Carrot Spread

Hot Artichoke Dip

1 envelope LIPTON® RECIPE SECRETS® Onion Soup Mix*
1 can (14 ounces) artichoke hearts, drained and chopped
1 cup HELLMANN'S® or BEST FOODS® Real Mayonnaise
1 container (8 ounces) sour cream
1 cup shredded Swiss or mozzarella cheese (about 4 ounces)

*Also terrific with LIPTON® RECIPE SECRETS® Savory Herb with Garlic, Golden Onion, or Onion Mushroom Soup Mix.

1. Preheat oven to 350°F. In 1-quart casserole, combine all ingredients.

2. Bake, uncovered, 30 minutes or until heated through.

3. Serve with your favorite dippers. *Makes 3 cups dip*

Cold Artichoke Dip: Omit Swiss cheese. Stir in, if desired, ¼ cup grated Parmesan cheese. Do not bake.

Recipe Tip: When serving hot dip for a party, try baking it in 2 smaller casseroles. When the first casserole is empty, replace it with the second one, fresh from the oven.

Prep Time: 5 minutes
Bake Time: 30 minutes

Mexicali Corn Salsa

1 jar (16 ounces) ORTEGA® Salsa-Thick & Chunky
1⅓ cups whole kernel corn
¼ cup finely chopped green bell pepper
¼ cup finely chopped red bell pepper
2 tablespoons chopped fresh cilantro (optional)

COMBINE salsa, corn, bell peppers and cilantro in medium bowl. Cover; refrigerate for at least 2 hours.

SERVE as a relish with meat or poultry or as a dip with tortilla chips.

Makes 3 cups

Hot Artichoke Dip

Black Bean Dip

¾ cup uncooked black beans, rinsed and sorted
1 tablespoon vegetable oil
1 large onion, chopped
3 cloves garlic, minced
½ cup thick and chunky salsa (medium or hot)
1 can (4 ounces) chopped mild or hot chili peppers, well drained
1 tablespoon lime juice
¼ teaspoon salt
¼ teaspoon black pepper
⅛ teaspoon hot pepper sauce
Sour cream
Tortilla chips

1. To quick soak beans, place beans in large saucepan; cover with 4 inches water. Bring to a boil over high heat. Boil 2 minutes. Remove from heat; cover. Let stand 1 hour; rinse and drain.

2. Add 2 cups fresh cold water. Bring to a boil; reduce heat. Cover and simmer 1½ hours or until beans are tender.

3. Heat oil in medium skillet over medium-high heat. Add onion and garlic. Cook and stir 3 minutes or until onion is tender.

4. Transfer onion and garlic to food processor. Add beans, salsa, chilies, lime juice, salt, black pepper and hot pepper sauce; process until almost smooth, scraping side of bowl occasionally.

5. Cover; refrigerate 2 hours to allow flavors to blend. Top with sour cream and serve with tortilla chips. Garnish, if desired. *Makes 3 cups dip*

Note: Substitute 1 can (15 ounces) black beans, drained, for dried beans and proceed with step 3, if desired.

Black Bean Dip

Cowboy Caviar

    Nonstick cooking spray
2 teaspoons olive oil
1 small eggplant (about ¾ pound), peeled and chopped
1 cup chopped onion
1 jalapeño pepper,* seeded and finely chopped (optional)
1 can (15 ounces) Mexican-style diced tomatoes, undrained
1 can (15 ounces) black-eyed peas, rinsed and drained
1 teaspoon ground cumin
½ cup minced fresh cilantro
    Tortilla chips

*Jalapeño peppers can sting and irritate the skin; wear rubber gloves when handling peppers and do not touch eyes. Wash hands after handling.

1. Coat large nonstick skillet with cooking spray. Add oil; heat over medium heat. Add eggplant, onion and jalapeño pepper, if desired; cook and stir 10 minutes or until vegetables are tender.

2. Stir in tomatoes with juice, black-eyed peas and cumin. Cook 5 minutes, stirring frequently. Remove from heat; stir in cilantro.

3. Serve with tortilla chips. *Makes 16 servings*

tip

Black-eyed peas (sometimes called cowpeas) are actually beans. Each small beige bean has a black circular mark, an "eye," on it's inner curve. Black-eyed peas are popular in the Southern United States, and they are an essential ingredient in the traditional New Year's dish of rice and black-eyed peas called "Hoppin' John."

Cowboy Caviar

Grilled Red Bell Pepper Dip

1 medium red bell pepper, stemmed, halved and seeded
1 cup ricotta cheese
4 ounces cream cheese
¼ cup grated Parmesan cheese
2 cloves garlic, minced
½ teaspoon Dijon mustard
¼ teaspoon salt
¼ teaspoon herbes de Provence*
    Mini pita pockets, fresh vegetables, Melba toast or pretzels

Substitute dash each rubbed sage, crushed dried rosemary, thyme, oregano, marjoram and basil for herbes de Provence, if desired.

1. Grill bell pepper halves, skin side down, on covered grill over medium coals 15 to 25 minutes or until skin is charred, without turning. Remove from grill and immediately place in bowl; cover and let stand 15 to 20 minutes. Remove skin with paring knife; discard.

2. Place bell pepper in food processor. Add cheeses, garlic, mustard, salt and herbes de Provence; cover and process until smooth. Serve with mini pita pockets or vegetables for dipping. *Makes about 2 cups dip*

tip

A similar bell pepper dip can be made using roasted sweet red bell peppers from a jar. Substitute one jar (about 12 ounces), drained, for the red bell pepper in the recipe above, and proceed with step 2.

Grilled Red Bell Pepper Dip

Chocolate Fruit Dip

1 container (8 ounces) vanilla lowfat yogurt
⅓ cup packed light brown sugar
1 tablespoon HERSHEY'S Cocoa
½ teaspoon vanilla extract
   Dash ground cinnamon
   Assorted fresh fruit, cut up

Combine all ingredients except fruit in small bowl; stir with whisk until smooth. Cover; refrigerate until well chilled. Serve with assorted fresh fruit. Cover and refrigerate leftover dip. *Makes 10 servings*

Garlic & Herb Dip

1 cup sour cream
¼ cup mayonnaise
2 tablespoons chopped green onion
1 teaspoon dried basil
½ teaspoon dried tarragon
1 clove garlic, minced
¼ teaspoon salt
¼ teaspoon black pepper
   Assorted fresh vegetable dippers or pita chips

Blend all ingredients except dippers in medium bowl. Cover; refrigerate several hours or overnight. Serve with dippers. *Makes about 1¼ cups*

Chocolate Fruit Dip

Spicy Thai Satay Dip

⅓ cup peanut butter
⅓ cup *French's*® Honey Dijon Mustard
⅓ cup fat-free chicken broth
1 tablespoon chopped peeled fresh ginger
1 tablespoon honey
1 tablespoon *Frank's*® *RedHot*® Cayenne Pepper Sauce
1 tablespoon teriyaki sauce
1 tablespoon grated orange peel
2 cloves garlic, minced

1. Combine all ingredients in large bowl. Cover and refrigerate.

2. Serve with vegetables, chips or grilled meats.   *Makes 4 (¼-cup) servings*

Prep Time: 10 minutes

Vegetable-Topped Hummus

1 can (about 15 ounces) chick-peas, rinsed and drained
2 tablespoons tahini*
2 tablespoons lemon juice
1 clove garlic
¾ teaspoon salt
1 tomato, finely chopped
2 green onions, finely chopped
2 tablespoons chopped fresh parsley
  Pita bread wedges or assorted crackers

*Tahini is a thick paste made of ground sesame seed which is used in Middle Eastern cooking.

1. Combine chick-peas, tahini, lemon juice, garlic and salt in food processor or blender; process until smooth.

2. Combine tomato, onions and parsley in small bowl.

3. Place chick-pea mixture in medium serving bowl; spoon tomato mixture evenly over top. Serve with pita bread wedges or assorted crackers.   *Makes 8 servings*

Spicy Thai Satay Dip

Guacamole

2 large avocados, cut in half
¼ cup finely chopped tomato
2 tablespoons lime juice or lemon juice
2 tablespoons grated onion with juice
½ teaspoon salt
¼ teaspoon hot pepper sauce
Black pepper
Additional chopped tomato (optional)

Scoop avocado flesh into medium bowl; mash coarsely with fork. Stir in tomato, lime juice, onion with juice, salt and pepper sauce; mix well. Season with black pepper. Spoon into serving container. Serve immediately or cover and refrigerate up to 2 hours. Garnish with additional chopped tomato, if desired.   *Makes 2 cups*

Tip: To ripen hard avocados, store them in a loosely closed paper bag at room temperature for a few days.

Shrimp Dip with Crudités

1 can (6 ounces) small shrimp, drained and divided
½ cup cream cheese, softened
⅓ cup plus 1 tablespoon thinly sliced green onions, divided
3 tablespoons Caesar salad dressing
2 teaspoons prepared horseradish
¼ teaspoon salt
Assorted raw vegetables
Crispbread, Melba toast or other crackers

1. Reserve several shrimp for garnish. Combine remaining shrimp, cream cheese, ⅓ cup green onions, salad dressing, horseradish and salt in medium bowl; mix well. Transfer to serving dish; top with reserved shrimp and remaining 1 tablespoon green onions. Cover; chill at least 30 minutes before serving.

2. Serve with vegetables and crackers.   *Makes 10 servings*

Guacamole

Roasted Red Pepper Spread

1 cup roasted red peppers, rinsed and drained
1 package (8 ounces) cream cheese, softened
1 packet (1 ounce) HIDDEN VALLEY® The Original Ranch® Salad
Dressing & Seasoning Mix
Baguette slices and sliced ripe olives (optional)

Blot dry red peppers. In a food processor fitted with a metal blade, combine peppers, cream cheese and salad dressing & seasoning mix; process until smooth. Spread on baguette slices and garnish with olives, if desired. *Makes 2 cups*

Creamy Dill Veggie Dip

4 ounces cream cheese
½ package dry ranch salad dressing mix (about 2 tablespoons)
2 tablespoons milk
1½ teaspoons dried dill weed *or* 1 tablespoon chopped fresh dill
4 cups raw vegetables (such as cherry tomatoes, celery sticks, baby
carrots, broccoli florets, cucumber slices, zucchini slices and/or
red or green bell pepper strips)
8 unsalted breadsticks

1. Place cream cheese, dressing mix, milk and dill weed in blender; blend until smooth. Store, tightly sealed, in refrigerator.

2. Serve dip with vegetables and breadsticks. *Makes 8 servings*

Note: This recipe can be doubled, if needed.

Roasted Red Pepper Spread

Original Ranch® Spinach Dip

1 container (16 ounces) sour cream (2 cups)
1 box (10 ounces) frozen chopped spinach, thawed and squeezed dry
1 can (8 ounces) water chestnuts, rinsed, drained and chopped
1 packet (1 ounce) HIDDEN VALLEY® The Original Ranch® Salad Dressing & Seasoning Mix
1 loaf round French bread
Fresh vegetables, for dipping

Stir together sour cream, spinach, water chestnuts and salad dressing & seasoning mix. Chill 30 minutes. Just before serving, cut top off bread and remove center, reserving firm bread pieces. Fill bread bowl with dip. Cut reserved bread into cubes. Serve dip with bread and vegetables. *Makes 2½ cups*

Cheesy Mustard Dip

1 container (8 ounces) whipped cream cheese
¼ cup milk
3 tablespoons French's® Bold n' Spicy Brown Mustard or Sweet & Tangy Honey Mustard
2 tablespoons mayonnaise
2 tablespoons minced green onions

Combine ingredients for dip in medium bowl; mix until well blended.
Makes 8 servings (about 1¼ cups dip)

Prep Time: 15 minutes

Original Ranch® Spinach Dip

Hidden Valley® Bacon-Cheddar Ranch Dip

1 container (16 ounces) sour cream (2 cups)
1 packet (1 ounce) HIDDEN VALLEY® The Original Ranch® Dips Mix
1 cup (4 ounces) shredded Cheddar cheese
¼ cup crisp-cooked, crumbled bacon*
 Potato chips or corn chips, for dipping

*Bacon pieces can be used.

Combine sour cream and dips mix. Stir in cheese and bacon. Garnish as desired. Chill at least 1 hour. Serve with chips. *Makes about 3 cups*

Louisiana Crab Dip with Crudités

1 package (8 ounces) cream cheese, softened
½ cup sour cream
3 tablespoons horseradish
2 tablespoons chopped fresh parsley
1 tablespoon coarse ground mustard
2 teaspoons TABASCO® brand Pepper Sauce
1 cup lump crabmeat
1 bunch baby carrots
1 bunch celery, cut into sticks
1 bunch asparagus spears, blanched
2 bunches endive
2 red/green bell peppers, cored and cut into strips

Blend cream cheese, sour cream, horseradish, parsley, mustard and TABASCO® Sauce in medium bowl until well mixed. Stir in crabmeat.

Arrange carrots, celery, asparagus, endive and peppers on large platter. Serve with dip. *Makes about 2 cups*

Hidden Valley® Bacon-Cheddar Ranch Dip

Asian Peanut Butter Dip

      3 tablespoons creamy peanut butter
      2 tablespoons apple butter
      2 tablespoons milk
      1 tablespoon soy sauce
  1½ teaspoons lime juice
    10 ribs celery, cut into fourths

Combine peanut butter, apple butter, milk and soy sauce in small bowl; whisk together until very smooth. Store, tightly sealed, in refrigerator. Serve with celery.

Makes 5 servings

Cheesy Spinach Dip

      1 cup sour cream
      1 cup cottage cheese
      1 box (10 ounces) frozen chopped spinach, thawed and squeezed
         dry
      1 can (8 ounces) sliced water chestnuts, drained and chopped
      1 package (1.4 ounces) instant vegetable soup mix
  ¼ cup (1 ounce) grated Parmesan cheese
      2 tablespoons milk (plus additional milk if necessary)
  1½ teaspoons dried chives
         Cut-up raw vegetables and crackers

1. Combine sour cream, cottage cheese, spinach, water chestnuts, soup mix, Parmesan cheese, milk and chives in large bowl; mix well. Cover and refrigerate at least 2 hours or overnight.

2. Stir well before serving. Add more milk if dip is too thick. Serve with raw vegetables and crackers.

Makes about 3½ cups

Asian Peanut Butter Dip

Savory Seafood Spread

2 packages (8 ounces each) light cream cheese, softened
1 package (8 ounces) imitation crab meat, flaked
2 tablespoons minced green onion
1 tablespoon prepared horseradish
1 tablespoon *Frank's® RedHot®* Original Cayenne Pepper Sauce
1 teaspoon *French's®* Worcestershire Sauce
½ cup sliced almonds
 Paprika
 Crackers
 Vegetable dippers

1. Preheat oven to 375°F. Beat or process cream cheese in electric mixer or food processor until smooth and creamy. Add crab, onion, horseradish, **Frank's RedHot** Sauce and Worcestershire; beat or process until well blended.

2. Spread cream cheese mixture onto 9-inch pie plate. Top with almonds and sprinkle with paprika. Bake 20 minutes or until mixture is heated through and almonds are golden.

3. Serve with crackers or vegetable dippers. *Makes 3 cups spread*

Prep Time: 10 minutes
Cook Time: 20 minutes

Savory Seafood Spread

Cheese, Please

Nutty Bacon Cheeseball

1 package (8 ounces) cream cheese, softened
½ cup milk
2 cups (8 ounces) shredded sharp Cheddar cheese
2 cups (8 ounces) shredded Monterey Jack cheese
¼ cup (1 ounce) crumbled blue cheese
10 slices bacon, cooked, crumbled and divided
¾ cup finely chopped pecans, divided
¼ cup finely minced green onions (white parts only)
1 jar (2 ounces) diced pimiento, drained
   Salt and black pepper
¼ cup minced fresh parsley
1 tablespoon poppy seeds

1. Beat cream cheese and milk in large bowl with electric mixer at low speed until blended. Add cheeses. Beat at medium speed until well mixed. Add half of bacon, half of pecans, green onions, and pimiento. Beat at medium speed until well mixed. Add salt and pepper to taste. Transfer half of mixture to large piece of plastic wrap. Shape into ball; wrap tightly. Repeat with remaining mixture. Refrigerate at least 2 hours or until chilled.

2. Combine remaining bacon and pecans with parsley and poppy seeds in pie plate or large dinner plate. Remove plastic wrap from chilled cheese balls. Roll in bacon mixture until well coated. Wrap each ball tightly in plastic wrap; refrigerate until ready to serve, up to 24 hours. *Makes about 24 servings*

Nutty Bacon Cheeseball

Hidden Valley® Torta

2 packages (8 ounces each) cream cheese
1 packet (1 ounce) HIDDEN VALLEY® The Original Ranch® Salad
   Dressing & Seasoning Mix
1 jar (6 ounces) marinated artichoke hearts, drained and chopped
⅓ cup roasted red peppers, drained and chopped
3 tablespoons minced fresh parsley

Beat cream cheese and salad dressing & seasoning mix together in a medium bowl. In a separate bowl, stir together artichokes, peppers and parsley. In a 3-cup bowl lined with plastic wrap, alternate layers of cream cheese and vegetable mixtures, beginning and ending with a cheese layer.

Chill 4 hours or overnight. Invert on plate; remove plastic wrap. Serve with crackers.
Makes 10 to 12 servings

Celebration Cheese Ball

2 packages (8 ounces each) cream cheese, softened
⅓ cup mayonnaise
¼ cup grated Parmesan cheese
2 tablespoons finely chopped carrot
1 tablespoon finely chopped red onion
1½ teaspoons prepared horseradish
¼ teaspoon salt
½ cup chopped pecans or walnuts
   Assorted crackers and breadsticks

Combine all ingredients except pecans and crackers in medium bowl. Cover and refrigerate until firm.

Shape cheese mixture into a ball; roll in pecans. Wrap cheese ball in plastic wrap and refrigerate at least 1 hour. Serve with assorted crackers and breadsticks.
Makes about 2½ cups

Hidden Valley® Torta

Zesty Cheese Fondue

1 package (1.8 ounces) white sauce mix
2 cups beer or nonalcoholic malt beverage
1 clove garlic, minced
1 package (16 ounces) pasteurized process cheese spread, cubed
3 tablespoons *Frank's® RedHot®* Original Cayenne Pepper Sauce
1 loaf French or Italian bread, cubed
Apple slices

1. Prepare white sauce mix in large saucepan according to package directions except substitute beer for milk and add garlic. Stir in cheese; cook, stirring constantly, until cheese melts and sauce is smooth. Stir in **Frank's RedHot** Sauce.

2. Transfer mixture to fondue pot or heated chafing dish. Serve warm with bread cubes or apple slices. *Makes 16 servings (4 cups)*

Prep Time: 15 minutes
Cook Time: 10 minutes

Honey-Nut Glazed Brie

8 ounces Brie cheese (wedge or round)
¼ cup I CAN'T BELIEVE IT'S NOT BUTTER!® Spread
1 cup coarsely chopped walnuts
¼ teaspoon ground cinnamon (optional)
⅛ teaspoon ground nutmeg (optional)
2 tablespoons honey
2 large green and/or red apples, cored and thinly sliced

Arrange cheese* on serving platter; set aside.

In 10-inch nonstick skillet, melt I Can't Believe It's Not Butter!® Spread over medium-high heat and stir in walnuts until coated. Stir in cinnamon and nutmeg until blended. Stir in honey and cook, stirring constantly, 2 minutes or until mixture is bubbling. Immediately pour over cheese. Serve hot with apples. *Makes 8 servings*

*If desired, on microwave-safe plate, arrange cheese and top with cooked nut mixture. Microwave at HIGH (Full Power) 1 minute or until cheese is warm. OR, in 1-quart shallow casserole, arrange cheese and top with cooked nut mixture. Bake at 350°F for 10 minutes or until Brie just begins to melt. Serve as above.

Zesty Cheese Fondue

Dreamy Orange Cheesecake Dip

    1 package (8 ounces) cream cheese, softened
  ½ cup orange marmalade
  ½ teaspoon vanilla
    2 cups whole strawberries
    2 cups cantaloupe chunks
    2 cups apple slices

1. Combine cream cheese, marmalade and vanilla in small bowl; mix well. Garnish with orange peel and mint leaves.

2. Serve with fruit dippers. *Makes 12 servings*

Note: Dip can be prepared ahead of time. Store, covered, in refrigerator for up to 2 days.

Easy Cheesy Artichoke & Spinach Bread

    1 can (14 ounces) artichoke hearts, drained and chopped
    1 package (10 ounces) frozen chopped spinach or chopped broccoli, thawed and squeezed dry
    1 cup HELLMANN'S® or BEST FOODS® Real Mayonnaise
    1 cup grated Parmesan cheese
    1 clove garlic, finely chopped or ¼ teaspoon LAWRY'S® Garlic Powder with Parsley (optional)
    1 loaf French or Italian bread (about 16 inches long), halved lengthwise

1. Preheat oven to 350°F.

2. In small bowl, combine all ingredients except bread; evenly spread on bread. Bake 12 minutes or until golden and heated through. *Makes 8 servings*

Prep Time: 10 minutes
Cook Time: 12 minutes

Dreamy Orange Cheesecake Dip

Cheese Twists

1 cup all-purpose flour
½ teaspoon baking soda
½ teaspoon salt
½ teaspoon dry mustard
⅛ teaspoon ground red pepper
¾ cup grated Parmesan cheese, divided
½ cup (1 stick) butter or margarine, softened
3 egg yolks
2 teaspoons water
1 egg white, lightly beaten
1 tablespoon sesame seeds (optional)

1. Preheat oven to 400°F. Grease two cookie sheets. Combine flour, baking soda, salt, mustard and red pepper in large bowl. Reserve 1 tablespoon cheese; stir remaining cheese into flour mixture. Cut in butter with pastry blender or 2 knives until mixture resembles fine crumbs. Add egg yolks and water, mixing until dough forms. Shape into a ball; flatten and wrap in plastic wrap. Refrigerate 2 hours or until firm.

2. Roll out dough on lightly floured surface into 12-inch square (about ⅛ inch thick). Brush surface lightly with egg white and sprinkle with remaining 1 tablespoon cheese and sesame seeds, if desired. Cut dough in half. Cut each half crosswise into ¼-inch strips. Twist 2 strips together. Repeat with remaining strips. Place 1 inch apart on prepared cookie sheets.

3. Bake 6 to 8 minutes or until light golden brown. Remove from cookie sheets and cool completely on wire racks. Store in airtight container.   *Makes 24 twists*

Variation: Prepare dough and cut as directed. Place ¾ of strips on cookie sheets. Form rings with remaining strips; seal edges. Place on cookie sheets. Bake and cool as directed. To serve, arrange 3 to 4 strips into small stacks. Insert stacks into rings.

Easiest Three-Cheese Fondue

2 cups (8 ounces) shredded mild or sharp Cheddar cheese
¾ cup reduced-fat (2%) milk
½ cup (2 ounces) crumbled blue cheese
1 package (3 ounces) cream cheese, cut into cubes
¼ cup finely chopped onion
1 tablespoon all-purpose flour
1 tablespoon butter or margarine
2 cloves garlic, minced
4 to 6 drops hot pepper sauce
⅛ teaspoon ground red pepper
Breadsticks and assorted fresh vegetables for dipping

Slow Cooker Directions

Combine all ingredients except breadsticks and vegetables in slow cooker. Cover and cook on LOW 2 to 2½ hours, stirring once or twice, until cheese is melted and smooth. Increase heat to HIGH and cook 1 to 1½ hours or until heated through. Serve with breadsticks and fresh vegetables. Garnish as desired.

Makes about 1½ cups dip

Lighten Up: To reduce the total fat, replace the Cheddar cheese and cream cheese with reduced-fat Cheddar and cream cheeses.

White Pizza Dip

1 envelope LIPTON® RECIPE SECRETS® Savory Herb with Garlic Soup Mix
1 container (16 ounces) sour cream
1 cup (8 ounces) ricotta cheese
1 cup shredded mozzarella cheese (about 4 ounces), divided
¼ cup (1 ounce) chopped pepperoni (optional)
1 loaf Italian or French bread, sliced

1. Preheat oven to 350°F. In shallow 1-quart casserole, combine soup mix, sour cream, ricotta cheese, ¾ cup mozzarella cheese and pepperoni.

2. Sprinkle with remaining ¼ cup mozzarella cheese.

3. Bake uncovered 30 minutes or until heated through. Serve with bread.

Makes 3 cups dip

Prep Time: 10 minutes
Cook Time: 30 minutes

tip

To keep hot dips hot, serve them in a small slow cooker or fondue pot. If you don't have either of those options, you might invest in a disposable aluminum chafing dish or even rent one for the day. Another simple trick is to divide the dip into two or more serving dishes, so you can keep an extra bowl of dip warmed and ready to easily replace the one that's cooling on the buffet table.

White Pizza Dip

Baked Apricot Brie

1 round (8 ounces) Brie cheese
⅓ cup apricot preserves
2 tablespoons sliced almonds
Assorted crackers

1. Preheat oven to 400°F. Place cheese in small baking pan. Spread top of cheese with preserves; sprinkle with almonds.

2. Bake about 10 to 12 minutes or until cheese begins to melt and lose its shape. Serve hot with crackers. Refrigerate leftovers; reheat before serving.

Makes 6 servings

Cook's Notes: Brie is a soft-ripened, unpressed cheese made from cow's milk. It has a distinctive round shape, edible white rind and creamy yellow interior. Avoid Brie that has a chalky center (it is underripe) or a strong ammonia odor (it is overripe). The cheese should give slightly to pressure and have an evenly colored, barely moist rind.

Cook Time: 12 minutes

tip

Many sweet accompaniments work well with cheese. If you prefer raspberry or fig preserves to apricot, feel free to adjust the recipe accordingly. If you choose not to bake your Brie, it's still important to bring it out of the refrigerator at least a half hour in advance and serve it at room temperature. Other delicious options to serve alongside Brie include fresh grapes, dried or fresh figs, sweet mango chutney and tart, crisp apple slices.

Baked Apricot Brie

Greek-Style Grilled Feta

1 package (8 ounces) feta cheese, sliced in half horizontally
24 (¼-inch-thick) slices small onion
½ green bell pepper, thinly sliced
½ red bell pepper, thinly sliced
½ teaspoon dried oregano
¼ teaspoon garlic pepper or black pepper
24 (½-inch-thick) slices French bread

1. Spray 14-inch-long sheet of foil with nonstick cooking spray. Cut feta into 24 slices. Place onion slices in center of foil and top with feta slices. Sprinkle with bell pepper slices, oregano and garlic pepper, leaving a 2-inch border around the food. Bring the two long sides together above the food; fold down in a series of locked folds, allowing some room for heat circulation and expansion. Fold the short ends up and over again. Press folds firmly to seal the foil packet.

2. Prepare grill for direct grilling. Place foil packet on grid upside down; grill on covered grill over medium coals about 15 minutes. Turn packet over; grill on covered grill 10 to 15 minutes more.

3. Open packet carefully. Serve immediately with slices of French bread.

Makes 8 servings

Greek-Style Grilled Feta

Chutney Cheese Spread

2 packages (8 ounces each) cream cheese, softened
1 cup (4 ounces) shredded Cheddar cheese
½ cup mango chutney
¼ cup thinly sliced green onions with tops
3 tablespoons dark raisins, chopped
2 cloves garlic, minced
1 to 1½ teaspoons curry powder
¾ teaspoon ground coriander
½ to ¾ teaspoon ground ginger
1 tablespoon chopped dry-roasted peanuts

1. Place cream cheese and Cheddar cheese in food processor or blender. Cover; process until smooth. Stir in chutney, green onions, raisins, garlic, curry powder, coriander and ginger to taste. Cover; refrigerate 2 to 3 hours.

2. Sprinkle spread with peanuts. Serve with additional green onions and melba toast, if desired. *Makes about 20 servings*

Cook's Tip: This spread can also be garnished with one tablespoon toasted coconut, lending a slightly sweeter flavor.

Beer Cheese Dip

2 cups shredded Cheddar cheese
2 packages (8 ounces each) cream cheese, softened
1 packet (1 ounce) HIDDEN VALLEY® The Original Ranch® Salad
Dressing & Seasoning Mix
½ to ¾ cup beer
Chopped green onion
Additional Cheddar cheese

In medium bowl, combine Cheddar cheese, cream cheese and salad dressing & seasoning mix. Gradually stir in beer until mixture is to desired consistency. Garnish with green onion and additional Cheddar cheese. Serve with pretzels or assorted fresh vegetables, if desired. *Makes about 3 cups*

Chutney Cheese Spread

Pesto Cheesecake

Crust
> **1 cup fine dry bread crumbs**
> **½ cup very finely chopped toasted pine nuts or walnuts**
> **3 tablespoons melted butter or margarine**

Filling
> **2 cups (15 ounces) SARGENTO® Light Ricotta Cheese**
> **½ cup half-and-half**
> **2 tablespoons all-purpose flour**
> **½ teaspoon salt**
> **2 eggs**
> **⅓ cup Homemade Pesto Sauce (recipe follows) or prepared pesto sauce**

Preheat oven to 350°F. Lightly grease sides of 8- or 9-inch springform pan.

Combine bread crumbs, nuts and butter in small bowl until well blended. Press evenly onto bottom of pan. Refrigerate until ready to use.

Combine Ricotta cheese, half-and-half, flour and salt in medium bowl with electric mixer. Beat at medium speed until smooth. Add eggs, one at a time; beat until smooth. Pour into prepared crust. Spoon pesto by teaspoonful randomly over cheese mixture. Gently swirl with knife for marbled effect.

Bake 45 minutes or until center is just set; turn off oven. Cool in oven with door open 30 minutes. Remove from oven. Cool completely on wire rack. Cut into thin slices before serving. *Makes 10 servings*

Homemade Pesto Sauce: In food processor or blender, mince 1 clove garlic. Add ½ cup packed fresh basil leaves and 1 tablespoon toasted pine nuts or walnuts. Process until smooth, scraping down side of bowl once. With machine running, drizzle 2 tablespoons olive oil into bowl; process until smooth. Add ¼ cup (1 ounce) SARGENTO® Fancy Parmesan Shredded Cheese; process just until cheese is blended.

Pesto Cheesecake

Wisconsin Edam and Beer Spread

4 cups shredded Wisconsin Edam Cheese*
¾ cup butter, cubed and softened
2 tablespoons snipped fresh chives
2 teaspoons Dijon mustard
½ cup amber or dark beer, at room temperature
   Cocktail rye or pumpernickel bread slices

Wisconsin Gouda can be substituted for Edam.

In large bowl, place shredded cheese, butter, chives and mustard; mix with spoon until blended. Stir in beer until blended. Chill until serving time. Serve as spread with cocktail bread.   *Makes 4 cups*

Variation: Cut one fifth from top of 2-pound Wisconsin Edam cheese ball to create flat surface. With butter curler or melon baller, remove cheese from center of ball, leaving ½-inch-thick shell. Shred enough of cheese removed from ball to measure 4 cups. Reserve remaining cheese for another use. Follow directions given above. Spoon spread into hollowed-out cheese ball; reserve remaining spread for refills. Chill until serving time.

Favorite recipe from **Wisconsin Milk Marketing Board**

Wisconsin Edam and Beer Spread

Quattro Formaggio Pizza

1 (12-inch) Italian bread shell
½ cup prepared pizza or marinara sauce
4 ounces shaved or thinly sliced provolone cheese
1 cup (4 ounces) shredded smoked or regular mozzarella cheese
2 ounces Asiago or brick cheese, thinly sliced
¼ cup freshly grated Parmesan or Romano cheese

1. Heat oven to 450°F. Place bread shell on baking sheet. Spread pizza sauce evenly over bread shell.

2. Top sauce with provolone, mozzarella, Asiago and Parmesan cheeses. Bake 14 minutes or until bread shell is golden brown and cheese is melted. Cut into wedges; serve immediately. *Makes 6 to 8 servings*

Serving Suggestion: Serve with a tossed green salad.

Prep and Cook Time: 26 minutes

tip

Pizza makes a great appetizer. In addition to traditional toppings as in the recipe above, you can try many variations, such as barbecued chicken, smoked salmon or grilled vegetables. Crust can be made from refrigerated biscuit dough, refrigerated crescent rolls or sturdy flatbreads.

Quattro Formaggio Pizza

Cheesy Snack Squares

1 ¼ cups all-purpose flour
¾ cup cornmeal
2 medium green onions, thinly sliced
4 teaspoons sugar
2 teaspoons baking powder
1 teaspoon Italian seasoning
¼ teaspoon salt
1 cup milk
¼ cup vegetable oil
1 egg
1 cup (4 ounces) shredded Cheddar cheese
¼ cup finely chopped green bell pepper
¼ cup finely chopped red bell pepper
2 slices crisp-cooked bacon, crumbled

1. Preheat oven to 400°F. Grease 11×7-inch baking dish.

2. Combine flour, cornmeal, green onions, sugar, baking powder, Italian seasoning and salt in large bowl; mix well. Combine milk, oil and egg in small bowl. Add to cornmeal mixture; mix just until moistened. Spread evenly in prepared dish. Combine cheese, bell peppers and bacon in medium bowl. Sprinkle evenly over cornmeal mixture.

3. Bake 25 to 30 minutes or until wooden toothpick inserted into center comes out clean. Let stand 10 minutes before cutting. *Makes about 15 appetizers*

Note: Also great as a side dish to fish, chicken or pork. Just cut into 8 squares.

BROILED CHICKEN

Cooking time: 15-20 mins.
Preparation time: 5-8 mins.
Main cooking utensil:
broiler pan

For 4 people you need:
4 joints of young chicken
2-4 tablespoons butter
seasoning
squeeze lemon juice
(optional)

Additional accompaniments:
whole or sliced mushrooms
whole or halved tomatoes
little butter
seasoning
bacon slices

1 Put joints of chicken on to grid of broiler pan if you can get this a reasonable distance away from the broiler. If your shelf is close to the broiler, then it is better to put the chicken in the actual broiler pan.
2 Brush with a little melted butter and season lightly; a squeeze of lemon juice adds flavor.
3 Heat the broiler and put the chicken under.
4 Allow 4-5 minutes on either side with the broiler at maximum heat.
5 Turn the heat lower and allow a further 8-12 minutes.
6 Broil sliced or whole mushrooms and/or tomatoes at the same time. Brush with melted butter and season. Add chopped or whole slices of bacon during cooking.

TO SERVE: On hot dish with accompaniments around or over top, and a green vegetable.

BROILED CHICKEN

Quattro Formaggio Pizza

Cheesy Snack Squares

1¼ cups all-purpose flour
¾ cup cornmeal
2 medium green onions, thinly sliced
4 teaspoons sugar
2 teaspoons baking powder
1 teaspoon Italian seasoning
¼ teaspoon salt
1 cup milk
¼ cup vegetable oil
1 egg
1 cup (4 ounces) shredded Cheddar cheese
¼ cup finely chopped green bell pepper
¼ cup finely chopped red bell pepper
2 slices crisp-cooked bacon, crumbled

1. Preheat oven to 400°F. Grease 11×7-inch baking dish.

2. Combine flour, cornmeal, green onions, sugar, baking powder, Italian seasoning and salt in large bowl; mix well. Combine milk, oil and egg in small bowl. Add to cornmeal mixture; mix just until moistened. Spread evenly in prepared dish. Combine cheese, bell peppers and bacon in medium bowl. Sprinkle evenly over cornmeal mixture.

3. Bake 25 to 30 minutes or until wooden toothpick inserted into center comes out clean. Let stand 10 minutes before cutting.   *Makes about 15 appetizers*

Note: Also great as a side dish to fish, chicken or pork. Just cut into 8 squares.

Cheesy Snack Squares

Tomato-Pesto Stuffed Brie

**1 cup boiling water
1 package (about 3 ounces) sun-dried tomatoes
4 tablespoons *Frank's®* *RedHot®* Original Cayenne Pepper Sauce
2 green onions, chopped
2 (5-inch) rounds Brie cheese, about 13 ounces each, well chilled
1 jar (1¾ ounces) pine nuts, toasted*
3 tablespoons butter, softened
¾ cup chopped fresh parsley**

*To toast pine nuts, bake at 350°F 5 minutes or until golden.

1. Pour boiling water over tomatoes in medium bowl. Let stand 4 minutes or until just softened; drain well and pat dry with paper towels. Place tomatoes, **Frank's RedHot** Sauce and onions in food processor; process until smooth paste forms.

2. Using large sharp knife, split each Brie round in half horizontally. Spread tomato mixture over cut sides of bottom halves. Sprinkle evenly with pine nuts. Cover bottom halves with top halves, cut side down. Press gently. Spread butter on edges of rounds; roll in chopped parsley. Refrigerate about 1 hour. Cut into wedges; serve with crackers or French bread.   *Makes 12 servings*

Note: Filled Brie may be served warm. (Do not coat with butter and parsley.) Place in baking dish; bake at 325°F 5 to 10 minutes or until slightly softened.

Prep Time: 30 minutes
Chill Time: 1 hour

Tomato-Pesto Stuffed Brie

Cream Cheese Dip with Vegetables

2 packages (8 ounces each) cream cheese, softened
⅔ cup mayonnaise
1 tablespoon coarse-grained Dijon mustard
⅓ cup finely chopped red onion
½ teaspoon dried parsley flakes
½ teaspoon black pepper
¼ teaspoon garlic powder
Red onion rings (optional)
Assorted fresh vegetables: bell pepper strips, broccoli florets, baby carrots, cucumber slices, pea pods, zucchini and summer squash slices

1. Beat cream cheese 1 minute in medium bowl with electric mixer at medium speed until smooth. Beat in mayonnaise and mustard until well blended. Stir in onion, parsley, black pepper and garlic powder.

2. Garnish dip with onion rings. Serve with vegetables.

Makes about 3 cups dip

tip

Choosing the freshest vegetables is even more important when you will be serving them raw as crudités. Purchase what is in season from a reputable produce market, or better yet a farmer's market. Think beyond the usual and try adding baby radishes with greens still attached, jicama or asparagus spears to your selection. Some items, such as broccoli, cauliflower and asparagus, look and taste better when blanched (cooked briefly in boiling water) before serving.

Cream Cheese Dip with Vegetables

Zesty Pesto Cheese Spread and Dip

2 packages (8 ounces each) cream cheese, softened
1 cup shredded mozzarella cheese
1 cup chopped fresh basil or parsley
½ cup grated Parmesan cheese
½ cup pine nuts, toasted
⅓ cup *French's®* *Gourmayo*™ Caesar Ranch
1 teaspoon minced garlic

1. Combine all ingredients in food processor. Cover and process until smooth and well blended.

2. Spoon pesto spread into serving bowl or crock. Spread on crackers or serve with vegetable crudités. *Makes about 3 cups*

Tip: To toast pine nuts, place nuts on baking sheet. Bake at 350°F for 8 to 10 minutes or until lightly golden or microwave on HIGH (100%) 1 minute.

Serving Suggestion: Use Pesto Spread as a filling in sandwich wraps or pipe into cherry tomatoes using a pastry bag filled with a decorative tip.

Prep Time: 15 minutes

Zesty Pesto Cheese Spread and Dip

Filled & Folded

Tuna in Crispy Won Ton Cups

18 won ton skins, each 3¼ inches square
Butter or olive oil cooking spray
1 (3-ounce) STARKIST Flavor Fresh Pouch® Tuna (Albacore or Chunk Light)
⅓ cup cold cooked orzo (rice-shaped pasta) or cooked rice
¼ cup southwestern ranch-style vegetable dip with jalapeños or other sour cream dip
¼ cup drained pimiento-stuffed green olives, chopped
3 tablespoons sweet pickle relish, drained
Paprika, for garnish
Parsley sprigs, for garnish

Cut won tons into circles with 3-inch round cookie cutter. Spray miniature muffin pans with cooking spray. Place one circle in each muffin cup; press to sides to mold won ton to cup. Spray each won ton with cooking spray. Bake in 350°F oven 6 to 8 minutes or until golden brown; set aside.

In small bowl, gently mix tuna, orzo, dip, olives and relish. Refrigerate filling until ready to serve. Remove won ton cups from muffin pan. Use rounded teaspoon to fill each cup; garnish with paprika and parsley.   *Makes 18 servings*

Tip: Cups may be made a day ahead; store in airtight container. Reheat in 350°F oven 1 to 2 minutes to recrisp.

Prep Time: 20 minutes

Tuna in Crispy Won Ton Cups

Chicken & Rice Puffs

1 box frozen puff pastry shells, thawed
1 package (about 6 ounces) long grain and wild rice
2 cups cubed cooked chicken
½ can (10¾ ounces) condensed cream of chicken soup, undiluted
⅓ cup chopped slivered almonds, toasted
⅓ cup diced celery
⅓ cup diced red bell pepper
⅓ cup chopped fresh parsley
¼ cup diced onion
¼ cup white wine or chicken broth
2 tablespoons half-and-half (optional)

1. Bake pastry shells according to package directions. Keep warm.

2. Prepare rice according to package directions.

3. Add remaining ingredients to rice; mix well. Cook over medium heat 4 to 5 minutes or until hot and bubbly. Fill pastry shells with rice mixture. Serve immediately.
Makes 6 servings

tip

Frozen puff pastry is easy to work with and handy to have on hand. Puff pastry shells, like the ones called for in the recipe above, are all ready to fill and bake. They can add elegance to just about any filling from creamed chicken to tuna salad. Just remember that a light crispy "puff" is caused by steam from the butter melting in between the layers of pastry. That's why you should never let puff pastry get too warm before baking.

Chicken & Rice Puffs

Honey Roasted Ham Biscuits

1 (10-ounce) can refrigerated buttermilk biscuits
2 cups (12 ounces) diced CURE 81® ham
½ cup honey mustard
¼ cup finely chopped honey roasted peanuts, divided

Heat oven to 400°F. Separate biscuits. Place in muffin pan cups, pressing gently into bottoms and up sides of cups. In bowl, combine ham, honey mustard and 2 tablespoons peanuts. Spoon ham mixture evenly into biscuit cups. Sprinkle with remaining 2 tablespoons peanuts. Bake 15 to 17 minutes. *Makes 10 servings*

Crab and Artichoke Stuffed Mushrooms

½ pound Florida blue crab meat
1 (14-ounce) can artichoke hearts, drained and finely chopped
1 cup mayonnaise*
½ cup grated Parmesan cheese
¼ teaspoon lemon pepper seasoning
⅛ teaspoon salt
⅛ teaspoon cayenne pepper
30 large fresh Florida mushrooms

*You can substitute mixture of ½ cup mayonnaise and ½ cup plain yogurt.

Remove any pieces of shell or cartilage from crab meat. Combine crab meat, artichoke hearts, mayonnaise, Parmesan cheese and seasonings; mix until well blended. Remove stems from mushrooms and fill cavities with crab meat mixture. Place in a lightly oiled, shallow baking dish. Bake in a preheated 400°F oven for 10 minutes or until hot and bubbly. *Makes 30 appetizer servings*

Favorite recipe from **Florida Department of Agriculture and Consumer Services, Bureau of Seafood and Aquaculture**

Honey Roasted Ham Biscuits

Mexican Roll-Ups

6 uncooked lasagna noodles
¾ cup prepared guacamole
¾ cup chunky salsa
¾ cup (3 ounces) shredded Cheddar cheese
Additional salsa (optional)

1. Cook lasagna noodles according to package directions. Rinse with cool water; drain. Cool.

2. Spread 2 tablespoons guacamole onto each noodle; top each with 2 tablespoons salsa and 2 tablespoons cheese.

3. Roll up noodles jelly-roll fashion. Cut each roll-up in half to form two equal-size roll-ups. Serve immediately with additional salsa, if desired, or cover with plastic wrap and refrigerate up to 3 hours. *Makes 12 appetizers*

Hummus-Stuffed Vegetables

1 can (15 ounces) chick-peas, rinsed and drained
1 medium clove garlic
1 tablespoon lemon juice
1 tablespoon olive oil
½ teaspoon ground cumin
¼ teaspoon salt
¼ teaspoon black pepper
1 cup snow peas (about 24)
¾ pound medium fresh mushrooms (about 24)

1. Combine chick-peas, garlic, lemon juice, oil, cumin, salt and pepper in food processor. Process until smooth. Transfer to pastry bag fitted with fluted tip.

2. Remove strings from pea pods. (Some pea pods will not have a stringy portion.) Carefully split pea pods with tip of paring knife. Remove stems from mushrooms; discard.

3. Pipe bean mixture into pea pods and into mushroom caps. Store loosely covered in refrigerator until ready to serve. *Makes about 48 appetizers*

Mexican Roll-Ups

Stuffed Mushroom Caps

2 packages (8 ounces each) fresh mushrooms
1 tablespoon butter
⅔ cup finely chopped cooked chicken
¼ cup grated Parmesan cheese
1 tablespoon chopped fresh basil
2 teaspoons lemon juice
⅛ teaspoon onion powder
⅛ teaspoon salt
Pinch pepper
Pinch garlic powder
1 small package (3 ounces) cream cheese, softened
Paprika

1. Preheat oven to 350°F. Clean mushrooms; remove stems and finely chop. Arrange mushroom caps, smooth side down, on greased baking sheet. Melt butter in medium skillet over medium-high heat and cook mushroom stems 5 minutes.

2. Add chicken, Parmesan cheese, basil, lemon juice, onion powder, salt, pepper and garlic powder to skillet. Cook and stir 5 minutes. Turn off heat and stir in cream cheese. Spoon mixture into hollow of each mushroom cap. Bake 10 to 15 minutes until heated through. Sprinkle with paprika.   *Makes about 26 stuffed mushrooms*

Stuffed Mushroom Caps

Chicken Rolls

2 teaspoons vegetable oil
1 package (10 ounces) frozen stir-fry vegetables
2 packages (8 ounces each) cooked diced chicken
1 tablespoon hot Asian chili sauce with garlic (optional)
1 tablespoon hoisin sauce
1 package (15½ ounces) refrigerated large crescent rolls
3 tablespoons orange marmalade
1 tablespoon plus 1 teaspoon white wine vinegar
1 tablespoon plus 1 teaspoon soy sauce

1. Preheat oven to 350°F.

2. Heat oil in large skillet. Add frozen vegetables; cook until liquid has evaporated, stirring frequently. Add chicken, chili sauce and hoisin sauce. Stir; remove from heat. Cool 5 minutes.

3. Separate crescent rolls on lightly floured board. Place ½ cup chicken filling on wide end of each roll; roll up to narrow point. Place rolls, seam side down, on ungreased baking sheet. Bake 18 to 20 minutes or until golden.

4. Combine orange marmalade, vinegar and soy sauce. Serve as dipping sauce with Chicken Rolls. *Makes 6 servings*

tip

Refrigerated crescent rolls are real time savers when it comes to making filled hor d'oeuvres. To make smaller versions of the recipe above, cut each crescent into two smaller triangles and adjust the amount of filling. Refrigerated biscuit dough is a handy shortcut, too. It can be rolled flat, pressed into muffin cups and baked to make pastry cups. For smaller cups, cut each biscuit into fourths before rolling into circles and pressing into mini muffin cups.

Chicken Roll

Cheese & Sausage Bundles

Salsa (recipe follows)
¼ pound bulk hot Italian pork sausage
1 cup (4 ounces) shredded Monterey Jack cheese
1 can (4 ounces) diced mild green chiles, drained
2 tablespoons finely chopped green onion
40 wonton wrappers
1 quart vegetable oil for deep frying

1. Prepare Salsa; set aside and keep warm. Brown sausage in small skillet over medium-high heat 6 to 8 minutes, stirring to separate meat. Drain fat.

2. Combine sausage, cheese, chiles and onion in medium bowl. Spoon 1 round teaspoon sausage mixture near 1 corner of wonton wrapper. Brush opposite corner with water. Fold corner over filling; roll into cylinder.

3. Moisten ends of roll with water. Bring ends together to make a "bundle," overlapping ends slightly; firmly press to seal. Repeat with remaining filling and wonton wrappers.

4. Heat oil in heavy 3-quart saucepan over medium heat until deep-fat thermometer registers 365°F. Fry bundles, a few at a time, about 1½ minutes or until golden. Adjust heat to maintain temperature. (Allow oil to return to 365°F between batches.) Drain on paper towels. Serve with Salsa. *Makes 40 appetizers*

Salsa

1 can (16 ounces) whole tomatoes, undrained
2 tablespoons olive oil
2 tablespoons chopped green onion
2 cloves garlic, minced
3 tablespoons chopped fresh cilantro or parsley

Combine tomatoes with juice and oil in food processor; process until chopped. Pour into 1-quart saucepan. Stir in green onion and garlic. Bring to a boil over medium heat. Cook, uncovered, 5 minutes. Remove from heat. Stir in cilantro.

Makes 1¾ cups salsa

Cheese & Sausage Bundles

Chicken Wraps

½ teaspoon Chinese 5-spice powder
½ pound boneless skinless chicken thighs
½ cup bean sprouts, rinsed well and drained
2 tablespoons minced green onion
2 tablespoons sliced almonds
2 tablespoons soy sauce
4 teaspoons hoisin sauce
1½ teaspoons hot chili sauce with garlic*
4 large leaves romaine or iceberg lettuce

*Hot chili sauce with garlic is available in the Asian foods section of most supermarkets.

1. Preheat oven to 350°F. Place chicken thighs on baking sheet; sprinkle with 5-spice powder. Bake 20 minutes or until chicken is cooked through. Dice chicken.

2. Place chicken in bowl. Add bean sprouts, green onion, almonds, soy sauce, hoisin sauce and chili sauce. Stir gently until combined. To serve, spoon ⅓ cup chicken mixture onto each lettuce leaf; roll or fold as desired.   *Makes 4 wraps*

Pesto-Stuffed Mushrooms

12 medium mushroom caps
⅔ cup prepared basil pesto
¼ cup (1 ounce) grated Parmesan cheese
¼ cup chopped roasted red pepper
3 tablespoons seasoned breadcrumbs
3 tablespoons pine nuts
¼ cup (1 ounce) shredded mozzarella cheese

1. Preheat oven to 400°F. Place mushroom caps, stem side up, on baking sheet.

2. Combine pesto, Parmesan cheese, red pepper, breadcrumbs and pine nuts in small bowl; mix until well blended.

3. Fill mushroom caps with pesto mixture. Sprinkle each with mozzarella cheese. Bake 8 to 10 minutes or until filling is hot and cheese is melted. Serve immediately.
Makes 12 mushrooms

Chicken Wrap

Pizza Snack Cups

1 can (12 ounces) refrigerated biscuits (10 biscuits)
½ pound ground beef
1 jar (14 ounces) RAGÚ® Pizza Quick® Sauce
½ cup shredded mozzarella cheese (about 2 ounces)

1. Preheat oven to 375°F. In muffin pan, evenly press each biscuit in bottom and up side of each cup; chill until ready to fill.

2. In 10-inch skillet, brown ground beef over medium-high heat; drain. Stir in Ragú Pizza Quick Sauce and heat through.

3. Evenly spoon beef mixture into prepared muffin cups. Bake 15 minutes. Sprinkle with cheese; bake an additional 5 minutes or until cheese is melted and biscuits are golden. Let stand 5 minutes. Gently remove pizza cups from muffin pan; serve.

Makes 10 pizza cups

Prep Time: 10 minutes
Cook Time: 25 minutes

Sausage Pinwheels

2 cups biscuit mix
½ cup milk
¼ cup butter or margarine, melted
1 pound BOB EVANS® Original Recipe Roll Sausage

Combine biscuit mix, milk and butter in large bowl until blended. Refrigerate 30 minutes. Divide dough into two portions. Roll out one portion on floured surface to ⅛-inch-thick rectangle, about 10×7 inches. Spread with half the sausage. Roll lengthwise into long roll. Repeat with remaining dough and sausage. Place rolls in freezer until firm enough to cut easily. Preheat oven to 400°F. Cut rolls into thin slices. Place on baking sheets. Bake 15 minutes or until golden brown. Serve hot. Refrigerate leftovers.

Makes 48 pinwheels

Note: This recipe may be doubled. Refreeze after slicing. When ready to serve, thaw slices in refrigerator and bake.

Pizza Snack Cups

Easy Sausage Empanadas

¼ pound bulk pork sausage
1 (15-ounce) package refrigerated pie crusts (2 crusts)
2 tablespoons finely chopped onion
⅛ teaspoon garlic powder
⅛ teaspoon ground cumin
⅛ teaspoon dried oregano, crushed
1 tablespoon chopped pimiento-stuffed olives
1 tablespoon chopped raisins
1 egg, separated

Let pie crusts stand at room temperature for 20 minutes or according to package directions. Crumble sausage into medium skillet. Add onion, garlic powder, cumin and oregano; cook over medium-high heat until sausage is no longer pink. Drain drippings. Stir in olives and raisins. Beat egg yolk slightly; stir into sausage mixture, mixing well. Carefully unfold crusts. Cut into desired shapes using 3-inch cookie cutters. Place about 2 teaspoons sausage filling on half the cutouts. Top with remaining cutouts. (Or, use round cutter, top with sausage filling and fold dough over to create half-moon shape.) Moisten fingers with water and pinch dough to seal edges. Slightly beat egg white; gently brush over tops of empanadas. Bake in 425°F oven 15 to 18 minutes or until golden brown.   *Makes 12 appetizer servings*

Prep Time: 25 minutes
Cook Time: 15 minutes

Favorite recipe from **National Pork Board**

Easy Sausage Empanadas

Ham and Cheese Strudels with Mustard Sauce

2 cups (12 ounces) diced CURE 81® ham
1 cup shredded Swiss cheese
1 cup sliced fresh mushrooms
1 egg, beaten
¼ cup chopped green onion
8 sheets frozen phyllo dough, thawed
½ cup butter or margarine, melted
Mustard Sauce (recipe follows)

Heat oven to 350°F. In bowl, combine ham, cheese, mushrooms, egg and green onion; mix well. Brush 1 sheet phyllo dough with butter. Keep remaining phyllo sheets covered with a dampened towel to prevent drying. To assemble, fold phyllo sheet in half crosswise; brush with butter. Fold in half crosswise again; brush with butter. Place ⅓ cup ham mixture in center of sheet. Fold long sides up and over filling, overlapping slightly. Fold into thirds from narrow edge. Place strudel, seam side down, on baking sheet. Cover with dampened towel to prevent drying. Repeat with remaining phyllo sheets, ham mixture and butter. Bake 20 minutes or until golden brown. Serve with Mustard Sauce. *Makes 8 servings*

Mustard Sauce: In saucepan, combine ½ cup sour cream, ½ cup mayonnaise or salad dressing, 2 tablespoons dry mustard and ½ teaspoon sugar. Heat over low heat, stirring occasionally, until warm.

Ham and Cheese Strudels with Mustard Sauce

Rice & Artichoke Phyllo Triangles

1 box UNCLE BEN'S® Butter & Herb Fast Cook Recipe Long Grain & Wild Rice
1 jar (6½ ounces) marinated quartered artichokes, drained and finely chopped
2 tablespoons grated Parmesan cheese
1 tablespoon minced onion or 1 green onion with top, finely chopped
⅓ cup plain yogurt or sour cream
10 sheets frozen phyllo dough, thawed

1. Prepare rice according to package directions. Cool completely.

2. Preheat oven to 375°F. In medium bowl, combine rice, artichokes, Parmesan cheese and onion; mix well. Stir in yogurt until well blended.

3. Place one sheet of phyllo dough on a damp kitchen towel. (Keep remaining dough covered.) Lightly spray dough with nonstick cooking spray. Fold dough in half by bringing short sides of dough together; spray lightly with additional cooking spray.

4. Cut dough into four equal strips, each about 3¼ inches wide. For each appetizer, spoon about 1 tablespoon rice mixture onto dough about 1 inch from end of each strip. Fold 1 corner over filling to make triangle. Continue folding as you would fold a flag to form a triangle that encloses filling. Repeat with remaining dough and filling.

5. Place triangles on greased baking sheets. Spray triangles with nonstick cooking spray. Bake 12 to 15 minutes or until golden brown. *Makes 40 appetizers*

Cook's Tips: To simplify preparation, the rice mixture can be prepared a day ahead, covered and refrigerated until ready to use. Use a pizza cutter to cut phyllo dough into strips.

Rice & Artichoke Phyllo Triangles

Almond Chicken Cups

1 tablespoon vegetable oil
½ cup chopped red bell pepper
½ cup chopped onion
2 cups chopped cooked chicken
⅔ cup prepared sweet-and-sour sauce
½ cup chopped almonds
2 tablespoons soy sauce
6 (6- to 7-inch) flour tortillas

1. Preheat oven to 400°F. Heat oil in small skillet over medium heat. Add bell pepper and onion. Cook and stir 3 minutes or until crisp-tender.

2. Combine vegetable mixture, chicken, sweet-and-sour sauce, almonds and soy sauce in medium bowl; mix until well blended.

3. Cut each tortilla in half. Place each half in 2¾-inch muffin cup. Fill each with about ¼ cup chicken mixture.

4. Bake 8 to 10 minutes or until tortilla edges are crisp and filling is hot. Remove muffin pan to cooling rack. Let stand 5 minutes before serving.

Makes 12 chicken cups

Prep and Cook Time: 30 minutes

Almond Chicken Cups

Stout Beef Bundles

 1 pound ground beef
 ½ cup sliced green onions
 1 medium clove garlic, minced
 ⅔ cup chopped water chestnuts
 ½ cup chopped red bell pepper
 ¼ cup stout
 2 tablespoons hoisin sauce
 1 tablespoon soy sauce
 2 tablespoons chopped fresh cilantro
 1 or 2 heads leaf lettuce, separated into leaves, outer leaves
     discarded

1. Brown ground beef in medium skillet over medium-high heat; drain fat. Add onions and garlic; cook and stir until tender. Stir in water chestnuts, bell pepper, stout, hoisin and soy sauce. Cook, stirring occasionally, until bell pepper is crisp-tender and most of liquid has evaporated. Remove from heat.

2. Stir in cilantro. Spoon ground beef mixture onto lettuce leaves; sprinkle with additional hoisin sauce, if desired. Wrap lettuce leaf around ground beef mixture to make bundle.   *Makes 8 servings*

Stout Beef Bundles

Tuna Quesadilla Stack

4 (10-inch) flour tortillas
¼ cup plus 2 tablespoons pinto or black bean dip
1 can (9 ounces) tuna packed in water, drained and flaked
2 cups (8 ounces) shredded Cheddar cheese
1 can (14½ ounces) diced tomatoes, drained
½ cup thinly sliced green onions
1½ teaspoons butter or margarine, melted

1. Preheat oven to 400°F.

2. Place 1 tortilla on 12-inch pizza pan. Spread with 2 tablespoons bean dip, leaving ½-inch border. Top with one third each of tuna, cheese, tomatoes and green onions. Repeat layers twice, beginning with tortilla and ending with onions.

3. Top with remaining tortilla, pressing gently. Brush with melted butter.

4. Bake 15 minutes or until cheese melts and top is lightly browned. Cool; cut into 8 wedges. *Makes 8 appetizers*

Tip: For a special touch, serve with assorted toppings, such as guacamole, sour cream and salsa.

Prep and Cook Time: 25 minutes

Tuna Quesadilla Stack

Pinwheel Appetizers

    3 cups cooked wild rice
    1 package (8 ounces) cream cheese
    ⅓ cup grated Parmesan cheese
    1 teaspoon dried parsley flakes
    ½ teaspoon garlic powder
    ½ teaspoon Dijon-style mustard
    2 to 3 drops hot pepper sauce (optional)
    3 (12-inch) soft flour tortillas
2½ ounces thinly sliced corned beef
    9 fresh spinach leaves

Combine wild rice, cream cheese, Parmesan cheese, parsley, garlic powder, mustard and pepper sauce. Spread evenly over tortillas, leaving ½-inch border on one side of each tortilla. Place single layer corned beef over rice and cheese mixture. Top with layer of spinach. Roll each tortilla tightly toward ½-inch border. Moisten border of tortilla with water; press to seal roll. Wrap tightly in plastic wrap. Refrigerate several hours or overnight. Cut into 1-inch slices to serve. *Makes 36 appetizers*

Favorite recipe from **Minnesota Cultivated Wild Rice Council**

tip

Flour tortillas can be rolled around a variety of fillings to make pinwheel appetizers. To add color and flavor try using flavored flour tortillas. They are often available in tomato flavor (red) and spinach flavor (green), among others.

Pinwheel Appetizers

Wings & Things

Can't Get Enough Chicken Wings

18 chicken wings (about 3 pounds)
  1 envelope LIPTON® RECIPE SECRETS® Savory Herb with
    Garlic Soup Mix
½ cup water
  2 to 3 tablespoons hot pepper sauce* (optional)
  2 tablespoons margarine or butter

*Use more or less hot pepper sauce as desired.

1. Cut tips off chicken wings (save tips for soup). Cut chicken wings in half at joint. Deep fry, bake or broil until golden brown and crunchy.

2. Meanwhile, in small saucepan, combine soup mix, water and hot pepper sauce. Cook over low heat, stirring occasionally, 2 minutes or until thickened. Remove from heat and stir in margarine.

3. In large bowl, toss cooked chicken wings with hot soup mixture until evenly coated. Serve, if desired, over greens with cut-up celery.   *Makes 36 appetizers*

Can't Get Enough Chicken Wings

Maple-Glazed Meatballs

1 ½ **cups ketchup**
1 cup maple syrup or maple-flavored syrup
⅓ cup soy sauce
1 tablespoon quick-cooking tapioca
1 ½ **teaspoons ground allspice**
1 teaspoon dry mustard
2 packages (about 16 ounces each) frozen fully-cooked meatballs
1 can (20 ounces) pineapple chunks in juice, drained

Slow Cooker Directions

1. Combine ketchup, maple syrup, soy sauce, tapioca, allspice and mustard in slow cooker.

2. Partially thaw and separate meatballs. Carefully stir meatballs and pineapple chunks into ketchup mixture.

3. Cover; cook on LOW 5 to 6 hours. Stir before serving. Serve with cocktail picks.

Makes about 48 meatballs

Variation: Serve over hot cooked rice for an entrée.

Prep Time: 10 minutes
Cook Time: 5 to 6 hours

Maple-Glazed Meatballs

Crispy Tuna Fritters

> **1 cup yellow corn bread mix**
> **¼ cup minced onion**
> **2 tablespoons minced pimiento**
> **¼ teaspoon salt**
> **⅛ teaspoon ground red pepper**
> **⅛ teaspoon black pepper**
> **¾ cup boiling water**
> **1 can (9 ounces) tuna packed in water, drained**
> **Vegetable oil**

1. Combine corn bread mix, onion, pimiento, salt, red pepper and black pepper in small bowl. Slowly stir in water. (Mixture will be thick.) Stir in tuna.

2. Pour oil into large skillet to depth of ½ inch; heat over medium heat until about 375°F on deep-fry thermometer.

3. Drop tuna mixture by tablespoonfuls into hot oil. Fry over medium heat 1 minute per side or until golden brown. Drain on paper towels.   *Makes 30 fritters*

Serving Suggestion: Serve fritters with cucumber ranch salad dressing or tartar sauce.

Prep and Cook Time: 30 minutes

tip

Fritters are small deep-fried cakes. They can be sweet or savory and are made by combining chopped food with a thick batter or dipping food into a batter before frying. Italian fritto misto, Japanese tempura and Indian pakora are examples of appetizer fritters from other cuisines.

Crispy Tuna Fritters

Savory Chicken Satay

1 envelope LIPTON® RECIPE SECRETS® Onion Soup Mix
¼ cup BERTOLLI® Olive Oil
2 tablespoons firmly packed brown sugar
2 tablespoons SKIPPY® Peanut Butter
1 pound boneless, skinless chicken breasts, pounded and cut into thin strips
12 to 16 large wooden skewers, soaked in water

1. In large plastic bag, combine soup mix, oil, brown sugar and peanut butter. Add chicken and toss to coat well. Close bag and marinate in refrigerator 30 minutes.

2. Remove chicken from marinade, discarding marinade. On skewers, thread chicken, weaving back and forth.

3. Grill or broil skewers until chicken is thoroughly cooked. Serve with your favorite dipping sauces. *Makes 12 to 16 appetizers*

Prep Time: 15 minutes
Marinate Time: 30 minutes
Cook Time: 8 minutes

Red Hot Pepper Wings

28 chicken wing drumettes (2¼ to 3 pounds)
2 tablespoons olive oil
Salt and black pepper
2 tablespoons melted butter
1 teaspoon sugar
¼ to ½ cup hot pepper sauce

Brush chicken with oil; sprinkle with salt and pepper. Grill chicken on covered grill over medium KINGSFORD® Briquets about 20 minutes until juices run clear, turning every 5 minutes. Combine butter, sugar and pepper sauce in large bowl; add chicken and toss to coat. Serve hot or cold. *Makes 28 wings*

Savory Chicken Satay

Summer Sausage Dippers

5 ounces sharp Cheddar cheese, cut into 1×½-inch chunks
32 pimiento-stuffed green olives
1 (9-ounce) HILLSHIRE FARM® Summer Sausage, cut into 32 thick
**   half-moon slices**
1 cup ketchup
½ cup apricot jam or preserves
1 tablespoon cider vinegar
2 teaspoons Worcestershire sauce

Secure 1 piece cheese and 1 olive onto 1 Summer Sausage slice with frilled toothpick; repeat with remaining cheese, olives and sausage. Arrange on platter. Cover and refrigerate until ready to serve. For dipping sauce, stir ketchup, jam, vinegar and Worcestershire sauce in small saucepan; heat over medium-low heat until warm and smooth. Serve sausage dippers with sauce.   *Makes 32 dippers*

Bandito Buffalo Wings

1 package (1.25 ounces) ORTEGA® Taco Seasoning Mix
12 (about 1 pound *total*) chicken wings
**   ORTEGA Salsa (any flavor)**

PREHEAT oven to 375°F. Lightly grease 13×9-inch baking pan.

PLACE seasoning mix in heavy-duty plastic or paper bag. Add 3 chicken wings; shake well to coat. Place wings in prepared pan. Repeat until all wings have been coated.

BAKE for 35 to 40 minutes or until juices run clear. Serve with salsa for dipping.
Makes 6 appetizer servings

Summer Sausage Dippers

Soy-Braised Chicken Wings

2 tablespoons soy sauce
2 tablespoons dry sherry
1 tablespoon sugar
1 tablespoon cornstarch
3 cloves garlic, minced, divided
1 teaspoon red pepper flakes
12 chicken wings (about 2½ pounds), tips removed and cut into
    halves
2 tablespoons vegetable oil
3 green onions with tops, cut into 1-inch pieces
¼ cup chicken broth
1 teaspoon sesame oil
1 tablespoon sesame seeds, toasted

1. For marinade, combine soy sauce, sherry, sugar, cornstarch, two-thirds of minced garlic and red pepper in large bowl; mix well. Stir in wing pieces; cover and marinate overnight in refrigerator, turning once or twice.

2. Drain chicken wings, reserving marinade. Heat large skillet over high heat 1 minute or until hot. Add vegetable oil and heat 30 seconds. Add half of wings; cook 10 to 15 minutes or until wings are brown on all sides, turning occasionally. Remove with slotted spoon to bowl; set aside. Reheat oil in wok 30 seconds and repeat with remaining wings. Reduce heat to medium. Pour off any remaining oil.

3. Add remaining garlic and onions to wok; cook and stir 30 seconds. Add wings and chicken broth. Cover and cook 5 minutes or until wings are tender, stirring occasionally to prevent wings from sticking to bottom of wok.

4. Add reserved marinade and stir-fry wings 1 minute until glazed with marinade. Add sesame oil; mix well. Transfer wings to serving platter; sprinkle with sesame seeds. Garnish, if desired. Serve immediately. *Makes 24 wings*

Soy-Braised Chicken Wings

Saucy Mini Franks

½ **cup** *French's®* **Sweet & Tangy Honey Mustard**
½ **cup chili sauce or ketchup**
½ **cup grape jelly**
1 **tablespoon** *Frank's®* *RedHot®* **Original Cayenne Pepper Sauce**
1 **pound mini cocktail franks or 1 pound cooked meatballs**

1. Combine mustard, chili sauce, grape jelly and **Frank's RedHot** Sauce in saucepan.

2. Add cocktail franks. Simmer and stir 5 minutes or until jelly is melted and franks are hot. *Makes about 6 servings*

Prep Time: 5 minutes
Cook Time: 5 minutes

Mussels Steamed in White Wine

¼ **cup olive oil**
1 **onion, chopped**
¼ **cup chopped celery**
2 **cloves garlic, minced**
1 **bay leaf**
½ **teaspoon dried basil leaves, crushed**
1 **pound raw mussels, scrubbed**
1 **cup dry white wine**
Chopped fresh parsley, for garnish

Heat oil in large saucepan. Add onion, celery, garlic, bay leaf and basil. Add mussels and wine; stir well. Cover and steam 4 to 6 minutes or until mussels open. Discard any mussels that do not open. Garnish with chopped parsley; serve.

Makes 2 servings

Favorite recipe from **National Fisheries Institute**

Saucy Mini Franks

Western Lamb Riblets

5 pounds lamb riblets, cut into serving-size pieces
¾ cup bottled chili sauce
½ cup beer
½ cup honey
¼ cup Worcestershire sauce
¼ cup finely chopped onion
1 clove garlic, minced
½ teaspoon crushed red pepper flakes

Trim excess fat from riblets. In saucepan, combine chili sauce, beer, honey, Worcestershire sauce, onion, garlic and pepper flakes. Bring mixture to a boil. Reduce heat; simmer, covered, 10 minutes. Remove from heat; cool.

Place riblets in resealable plastic food storage bag. Pour cooled marinade over riblets in bag. Close bag securely and refrigerate about 2 hours, turning bag occasionally to distribute marinade evenly.

Drain riblets; reserve marinade. Arrange medium-hot KINGSFORD® Briquets around drip pan. Place riblets on grid over drip pan. Cover grill; cook 45 minutes, turning riblets and brushing with marinade twice. Bring remaining marinade to a boil; boil 1 minute. Serve with riblets. *Makes 6 servings*

Piggy Wraps

1 package HILLSHIRE FARM® Lit'l Smokies
2 cans (8 ounces each) refrigerated crescent roll dough, cut into
small triangles

Preheat oven to 400°F.

Wrap individual Lit'l Smokies in dough triangles. Bake 5 minutes or until golden brown. *Makes about 50 hors d'oeuvres*

Note: Piggy Wraps may be frozen. To reheat in microwave, microwave at HIGH (100% power) 1½ minutes or at MEDIUM-HIGH (70% power) 2 minutes. When reheated in microwave, dough will not be crisp.

Western Lamb Riblets

Ginger Wings with Peach Dipping Sauce

Peach Dipping Sauce (recipe follows)
2 pounds chicken wings
¼ cup soy sauce
2 cloves garlic, minced
1 teaspoon ground ginger
¼ teaspoon white pepper

1. Preheat oven to 400°F. Line 15×10×1-inch jelly-roll pan with foil; set aside.

2. Prepare Peach Dipping Sauce; set aside.

3. Cut off and discard wing tips from chicken. Cut each wing in half at joint. Combine soy sauce, garlic, ginger and pepper in large bowl. Add chicken and stir until well coated. Place chicken in single layer in prepared pan. Bake 40 to 50 minutes or until browned, turning over halfway through cooking time. Serve hot with Peach Dipping Sauce. *Makes 6 appetizer servings*

Peach Dipping Sauce

½ cup peach preserves
2 tablespoons light corn syrup
1 teaspoon white vinegar
¼ teaspoon ground ginger
¾ teaspoon soy sauce

Combine preserves, corn syrup, vinegar and ginger in small saucepan. Cook and stir over medium-high heat until mixture simmers. Remove from heat; add soy sauce. Let cool. *Makes ½ cup sauce*

Ginger Wings with Peach Dipping Sauce

Barbecued Swedish Meatballs

Meatballs
   1½ **pounds lean ground beef**
      1 **cup finely chopped onions**
      ½ **cup fresh breadcrumbs**
      ½ **cup HOLLAND HOUSE® White Cooking Wine**
      1 **egg, beaten**
      ½ **teaspoon allspice**
      ½ **teaspoon nutmeg**

Sauce
      1 **jar (10 ounces) currant jelly**
      ½ **cup chili sauce**
      ¼ **cup HOLLAND HOUSE® White Cooking Wine**
      1 **tablespoon cornstarch**

Heat oven to 350°F. In medium bowl, combine all meatball ingredients; mix well. Shape into 1-inch balls. Place meatballs in 15×10×1-inch baking pan. Bake 20 minutes or until brown.

In medium saucepan, combine all sauce ingredients; mix well. Cook over medium heat until mixture boils and thickens, stirring occasionally. Add meatballs. To serve, place meatballs and sauce in fondue pot or chafing dish.   *Makes 6 to 8 servings*

Barbecued Swedish Meatballs

Tortilla Crunch Chicken Fingers

1 envelope LIPTON® RECIPE SECRETS® Savory Herb with Garlic Soup Mix
1 cup finely crushed plain tortilla chips or cornflakes (about 3 ounces)
1½ pounds boneless, skinless chicken breasts, cut into strips
1 egg
2 tablespoons water
2 tablespoons I CAN'T BELIEVE IT'S NOT BUTTER!® Spread, melted

1. Preheat oven to 400°F.

2. In medium bowl, combine savory herb with garlic soup mix and tortilla chips. In large plastic bag or bowl, combine chicken and egg beaten with water until evenly coated. Remove chicken and dip in tortilla mixture until evenly coated. On 15×10×1-inch jelly-roll pan sprayed with nonstick cooking spray, arrange chicken; drizzle with I Can't Believe It's Not Butter!® Spread. Bake, uncovered, 12 minutes or until chicken is thoroughly cooked. Serve with chunky salsa, if desired.

Makes about 24 chicken fingers

Tip: Serve chicken with your favorite fresh or prepared salsa.

tip

Breaded chicken or fish pieces make hearty and delicious appetizers. Experiment with different kinds of breading as suggested in the recipe above. Tortilla chips, crisp cereal and seasoned bread crumbs all work well. Dipping sauce can be a store-bought salsa, barbecue sauce, chili sauce or creamy salad dressing.

Tortilla Crunch Chicken Fingers

Lamb Meatballs with Tomato Mint Dip

  1½ **cups fine bulgur wheat**
    3 **cups cold water**
    2 **pounds ground American lamb**
    1 **cup minced fresh parsley**
    2 **medium onions, minced**
    1 **tablespoon salt**
   ½ **teaspoon ground black pepper**
   ½ **teaspoon ground allspice**
   ½ **teaspoon ground cinnamon**
   ½ **teaspoon ground nutmeg**
   ¼ **to** ½ **teaspoon ground red pepper (to taste)**
    1 **piece fresh ginger, about 2×1-inch, peeled and minced**
    1 **cup ice water**
     Tomato Mint Dip (recipe follows)

Place bulgar in medium bowl; pour cold water over bulgar to cover. Let soak about 10 minutes. Drain and place in fine meshed strainer; squeeze out water.

In large bowl, knead lamb with parsley, onions, seasonings and ginger. Add bulgur; knead well. Add enough ice water to keep mixture smooth. Use about 1 teaspoon meat mixture to make bite-sized meatballs. Place on ungreased jelly-roll pan. Bake in preheated 375°F oven 20 minutes. Meanwhile, prepare Tomato Mint Dip.

Place meatballs in serving bowl; keep warm. Serve hot with dip.

Makes 10 dozen meatballs

*Favorite recipe from **American Lamb Council***

Tomato Mint Dip

    2 **cans (15 ounces each) tomato sauce with tomato bits**
  1½ **teaspoons ground allspice**
    1 **teaspoon dried mint**

In small saucepan, heat all ingredients about 5 minutes to blend flavors.

*Favorite recipe from **American Lamb Council***

Crumb-Topped Clams

3 pounds live steamer or littleneck clams
4 slices bacon, cooked and crumbled, 2 tablespoons drippings reserved
⅓ cup finely chopped green onions
⅓ cup finely chopped fresh parsley
½ teaspoon grated lemon peel
2 tablespoons lemon juice
⅛ teaspoon hot pepper sauce
1 cup cracker crumbs
¼ cup grated Parmesan cheese

1. Tap clams and discard any that do not close. Scrub clams. Fill large saucepan or deep skillet with ½ inch of water; bring to a boil. Add clams; cover and steam just until shells pop open, about 2 minutes. Transfer to baking sheet. Discard top shells. Loosen clams in shells and replace in juices in bottom of shells.

2. Preheat oven to 400°F. In medium saucepan, cook and stir green onions and parsley in reserved bacon drippings until tender, about 1 minute. Remove from heat; add lemon peel, lemon juice and hot pepper sauce. Stir in cracker crumbs, Parmesan cheese and crumbled bacon.

3. Using teaspoon, mound crumb mixture over clams, pressing gently. Bake clams 5 minutes or until crumbs are golden brown. *Makes about 36 clams*

Variation: Scrub shells and remove top shell from 2 dozen fresh oysters. Loosen oysters from bottom of shells. Arrange on baking sheet. Prepare crumb topping as directed and spoon over oysters, pressing gently. Bake at 400°F about 8 minutes or until oysters are just cooked and crumbs are golden brown. Makes 24 oysters.

Buffalo Chicken Wing Sampler

2½ pounds chicken wing pieces
½ cup *Frank's*® *RedHot*® Original Cayenne Pepper Sauce
⅓ cup melted butter

1. Deep-fry* wings in hot oil (400°F) for 12 minutes until fully cooked and crispy; drain.

2. Combine **Frank's RedHot** Sauce and butter. Dip wings in sauce to coat.

3. Serve wings with celery and blue cheese dressing if desired.

Makes 8 appetizer servings

*For equally crispy wings, bake 1 hour at 425°F, or grill 30 minutes over medium heat.

***RedHot*® Sampler Variations:** Add one of the following to **RedHot** butter mixture; heat through. Tex-Mex: 1 tablespoon chili powder, ¼ teaspoon garlic powder. Asian: 2 tablespoons honey, 2 tablespoons teriyaki sauce, 2 teaspoons ground ginger. Sprinkle wings with 1 tablespoon sesame seeds. Zesty Honey-Dijon: Substitute the following blend instead of the **RedHot** butter mixture: ¼ cup each **Frank's*® *RedHot*®** Sauce, **French's*®** Honey Dijon Mustard and honey.

Prep Time: 5 minutes
Cook Time: 12 minutes

Potato Skins

4 baked potatoes, quartered
¼ cup sour cream
1 packet (1 ounce) HIDDEN VALLEY® The Original Ranch® Salad
**   Dressing & Seasoning Mix**
1 cup (4 ounces) shredded Cheddar cheese
**   Sliced green onions and/or bacon pieces* (optional)**

*Crisp-cooked, crumbled bacon can be used.

Scoop potato out of skins; combine potatoes with sour cream and salad dressing & seasoning mix. Fill skins with mixture. Sprinkle with cheese. Bake at 375°F. for 12 to 15 minutes or until cheese is melted. Garnish with green onions and/or bacon bits, if desired.

Makes 8 to 10 servings

Buffalo Chicken Wing Sampler

Coconut Chicken Tenders with Spicy Mango Salsa

1 firm ripe mango, peeled, seeded and chopped
½ cup chopped red bell pepper
3 tablespoons chopped green onion
2 tablespoons chopped fresh cilantro
Salt and ground red pepper
1½ cups flaked coconut
1 egg
1 tablespoon vegetable oil
¾ pound chicken tenders

1. Combine mango, bell pepper, onion and cilantro in small bowl. Season to taste with salt and ground red pepper. Transfer half of salsa to food processor; process until finely chopped (almost puréed). Combine with remaining salsa.

2. Preheat oven to 400°F. Spread coconut on large baking sheet. Bake 5 to 6 minutes or until lightly browned, stirring every 2 minutes. Transfer coconut to food processor; process until finely chopped but not pasty.

3. Beat egg with oil and pinch of ground red pepper in small bowl. Add chicken tenders; toss to coat. Roll tenders in coconut; arrange on foil-lined baking sheet. Bake 18 to 20 minutes or until no longer pink in center. Serve with Spicy Mango Salsa.

Makes 5 to 6 servings

Coconut Chicken Tenders with Spicy Mango Salsa

Barbecued Ribs

3 to 4 pounds pork baby back ribs
⅓ cup hoisin sauce
4 tablespoons soy sauce, divided
3 tablespoons dry sherry
3 cloves garlic, minced
2 tablespoons honey
1 tablespoon dark sesame oil

1. Place ribs in large resealable plastic food storage bag. Combine hoisin sauce, 3 tablespoons soy sauce, sherry and garlic; pour over ribs. Seal bag; turn to coat. Marinate in refrigerator at least 4 hours or up to 24 hours.

2. Preheat oven to 375°F. Drain ribs; reserve marinade. Place ribs on rack in shallow, foil-lined roasting pan. Bake 30 minutes. Turn; brush ribs with half of reserved marinade. Bake 15 minutes. Turn ribs over; brush with remaining marinade. Bake 15 minutes.

3. Combine remaining 1 tablespoon soy sauce, honey and sesame oil in small bowl; brush over ribs. Bake 5 to 10 minutes or until ribs are cooked through, browned and crisp.* Cut into serving-size pieces.   *Makes 8 servings*

Ribs may be made ahead to this point. Cover and refrigerate up to 3 days. To reheat, wrap ribs in foil; cook in preheated 350°F oven 40 minutes or until heated through. Cut into serving-size pieces.

Barbecued Ribs

Garlicky Gilroy Chicken Wings

2 pounds chicken wings (about 15 wings)
2 heads garlic, separated into cloves and peeled*
1 cup olive oil plus additional for greasing
1 teaspoon hot pepper sauce
1 cup grated Parmesan cheese
1 cup Italian-style bread crumbs
1 teaspoon black pepper
Celery slices for garnish

*To peel whole heads of garlic, drop garlic heads into enough boiling water in small saucepan to cover for 5 to 10 seconds. Immediately remove garlic with slotted spoon. Plunge garlic into cold water; drain. Peel away skins.

1. Preheat oven to 375°F.

2. Cut off and discard wing tips. Cut each wing in half at joint. Rinse wings and pat dry with paper towels.

3. Place garlic, 1 cup oil and hot pepper sauce in food processor; cover and process until smooth. Pour garlic mixture into small bowl. Combine cheese, bread crumbs and black pepper in shallow dish. Dip wings, one at a time, into garlic mixture, then roll in crumb mixture, coating evenly and shaking off excess.

4. Grease 13×9-inch nonstick baking pan; arrange wings in single layer in pan. Drizzle remaining garlic mixture over wings; sprinkle with remaining crumb mixture. Bake 45 to 60 minutes or until wings are brown and crisp. Garnish, if desired.

Makes about 30 pieces

Garlicky Gilroy Chicken Wings

International Nibbles

Nachos con Queso y Cerveza

    4 ounces tortilla chips
    Nonstick cooking spray
¾ cup chopped red onion
2 jalapeño peppers,* seeded and chopped
3 cloves garlic, finely chopped
2 teaspoons chili powder
½ teaspoon ground cumin
2 boneless skinless chicken breasts (about 8 ounces), cooked and
    chopped
1 can (14½ ounces) Mexican-style diced tomatoes, drained
⅓ cup pilsner lager beer
1 cup (4 ounces) shredded Monterey Jack cheese
2 tablespoons chopped black olives

*Jalapeño peppers can sting and irritate the skin. Wear rubber gloves when handling peppers and do not touch eyes. Wash hands after handling.

1. Preheat oven to 350°F. Place chips in 13×9-inch baking pan; set aside.

2. Spray large nonstick skillet with cooking spray. Heat over medium heat until hot. Add onion, peppers, garlic, chili powder and cumin. Cook 5 minutes or until vegetables are tender, stirring occasionally. Stir in chicken, tomatoes and pilsner. Simmer until liquid is absorbed.

3. Spoon chicken-tomato mixture over chips; top with cheese and olives. Bake 5 minutes or until cheese melts. Serve immediately. *Makes 4 servings*

Nachos con Queso y Cerveza

Marinated Roasted Pepper Tapas

1 large red bell pepper
1 large yellow bell pepper
3 tablespoons olive oil
1 tablespoon sherry wine vinegar or white wine vinegar
1 tablespoon capers, rinsed and drained
1 teaspoon sugar
1 clove garlic, sliced
½ teaspoon cumin seeds
1 loaf French bread

1. Cover broiler pan with foil. Preheat broiler. Place peppers on foil. Broil, 4 inches from heat source, 15 to 20 minutes or until blackened on all sides, turning peppers every 5 minutes with tongs. Place peppers in paper bag for 30 minutes.

2. Place oil, vinegar, capers, sugar, garlic and cumin seeds in small bowl. Whisk until combined.

3. Peel, core and seed peppers; cut into 1-inch square pieces. Place in resealable plastic food storage bag.

4. Pour oil mixture over peppers. Cover and refrigerate at least 2 hours or overnight, turning occasionally. Bring to room temperature before serving.

5. Slice bread into rounds; toast, if desired. Arrange peppers on top of rounds.

Makes 4 to 6 appetizer servings

Marinated Roasted Pepper Tapas

Falafel with Garlic Tahini Sauce

¾ cup uncooked dried chick-peas, rinsed and sorted
½ cup uncooked bulgur wheat
   Garlic Tahini Sauce (recipe on facing page)
1½ cups coarsely crumbled whole wheat bread
½ cup water
¼ cup fresh lemon juice
3 tablespoons chopped fresh cilantro
2 cloves garlic, minced
1 teaspoon ground cumin
½ teaspoon salt
½ teaspoon red pepper flakes
   Vegetable oil

1. To quick soak chick-peas, place in medium saucepan; cover with 4 inches water. Bring to a boil and cook 2 minutes. Remove from heat. Cover and let stand 1 hour. Drain chick-peas and discard water. To cook chick-peas, place in large saucepan and cover with 4 cups water. Bring to a boil; reduce heat to low. Cover; simmer 1½ to 2 hours or until tender. Rinse; drain and set aside. Meanwhile, prepare bulgur according to package directions; set aside. Prepare Garlic Tahini Sauce; set aside.

2. Place bread in small baking pan. Pour ½ cup water over bread and let stand 15 minutes or until water is absorbed. Squeeze water from bread.

3. Place chick-peas, lemon juice, cilantro, garlic, cumin, salt and red pepper in food processor; process until smooth. Add bread and bulgur to food processor; process until combined. Shape falafel mixture into 1½-inch balls. Place on baking sheet lined with waxed paper. Dry at room temperature 1 hour.

4. Heat 2 to 3 inches oil in large heavy Dutch oven over medium-high heat. Carefully add falafel to skillet; cook 3 to 3½ minutes until golden brown. Remove falafel with slotted spoon and place on paper towels to drain. Serve with Garlic Tahini Sauce.

Makes 8 to 10 servings

Garlic Tahini Sauce

½ cup plain yogurt
¼ cup tahini*
3 tablespoons water
2 tablespoons fresh lemon juice
1 clove garlic, minced
½ teaspoon cumin
    Salt and black pepper to taste

*Tahini is a thick paste made from ground sesame seeds and is used in Middle Eastern cooking. It is available in many large supermarkets.

Combine all ingredients in small bowl. Stir with wire whisk until well blended. Cover; refrigerate 1 hour.

Makes about 1 cup

Zesty Bruschetta

1 envelope LIPTON® RECIPE SECRETS® Savory Herb with
    Garlic Soup Mix
6 tablespoons BERTOLLI® Olive Oil*
1 loaf French or Italian bread (about 18 inches long), sliced
    lengthwise
2 tablespoons shredded or grated Parmesan cheese

*Substitution: Use ½ cup margarine or butter, melted.

Preheat oven to 350°F. Blend savory herb with garlic soup mix and oil. Brush onto bread, then sprinkle with cheese.

Bake 12 minutes or until golden. Slice, then serve.

Makes 1 loaf, about 18 pieces

Sopes

4 cups masa harina* flour
½ cup vegetable shortening or lard
2½ cups warm water
1 can (7 ounces) ORTEGA® Diced Green Chiles
2 tablespoons vegetable oil, *divided*
    Toppings: warmed ORTEGA Refried Beans, shredded mild
        Cheddar or shredded Monterey Jack cheese, ORTEGA Salsa (any
        flavor), sour cream, ORTEGA Sliced Jalapeños

*Masa harina is a type of corn flour used to make tortillas and other Mexican breads. It is available in the ethnic section of most large supermarkets.

PLACE masa harina flour in large bowl; cut in vegetable shortening with pastry blender or two knives until mixture resembles coarse crumbs. Gradually add water, kneading until smooth. Add chiles; mix well. Form dough into 35 small balls. Pat each ball into 3-inch patty; place on waxed paper.

HEAT 1 teaspoon oil in large skillet over medium-high heat for 1 to 2 minutes. Cook patties for 3 minutes on each side or until golden brown, adding additional oil as needed.

TOP with beans, cheese, salsa, dollop of sour cream and jalapeños.

Makes about 35 appetizers

Sopes

Meat-Filled Samosas

1 cup all-purpose flour
1 cup whole wheat flour
1¼ teaspoons salt, divided
2 tablespoons plus 2 teaspoons vegetable oil, divided
⅓ to ½ cup water
1 small onion, finely chopped
2 cloves garlic, minced
1 teaspoon finely chopped fresh ginger
¾ pound ground lamb or ground beef
2 teaspoons garam masala*
¾ cup frozen peas
1 small tomato, peeled, seeded and chopped
1 jalapeño pepper, seeded and chopped
2 teaspoons finely chopped fresh cilantro
Additional vegetable oil for frying
Cilantro Chutney, optional (recipe on facing page)

Garam masala is an Indian spice blend which includes cinnamon, coriander, cardamom and black pepper.

1. Combine flours and ½ teaspoon salt in large bowl. Stir in 2 tablespoons oil with fork; mix until mixture resembles fine crumbs. Gradually stir in enough water, about ⅓ cup, until dough forms a ball and is no longer sticky. Place dough on lightly floured surface; flatten slightly. Knead dough 5 minutes or until smooth and elastic. Divide dough in half and form 2 ropes, each about 9 inches long and 1 inch thick. Wrap in plastic wrap; let stand 1 hour.

2. Meanwhile, heat remaining 2 teaspoons oil in large skillet over medium heat. Add onion, garlic and ginger; cook and stir 5 minutes or until onion is softened. Crumble meat into skillet; cook 6 to 8 minutes or until browned, stirring to separate meat. Drain fat. Stir in garam masala and remaining ¾ teaspoon salt. Add peas, tomato, jalapeño and cilantro to skillet; mix well. Cover and cook 5 minutes or until peas are heated through. Cool to room temperature before filling samosas.

3. To form samosas, divide each rope of dough into 9 equal portions. Roll each piece on lightly floured surface into 4- to 5-inch round. Keep remaining dough pieces wrapped in plastic wrap to prevent drying. Cut each round of dough in half, forming 2 semi-circles. Moisten straight edge of 1 semi-circle with water and fold in half; press moistened edges together to seal. Spread dough apart to form cone; fill with 2 teaspoons meat filling. Press meat mixture into cone, leaving ½ inch of dough

above meat mixture. Moisten edges of dough and press firmly together. Place samosas on work surface and seal edges with fork.

4. Heat 3 to 4 inches oil in large heavy skillet over medium-high heat to 375°F on deep-fat thermometer. Cook 4 to 6 samosas at a time 3 to 4 minutes or until crisp and golden. Drain on paper towels. Serve with Cilantro Chutney, if desired.

Makes 36 samosas

Cilantro Chutney

- ½ cup green onions, cut into ½-inch lengths
- 1 to 2 jalapeño peppers,* seeded and coarsely chopped
- 2 tablespoons chopped fresh ginger
- 2 cloves garlic, peeled
- 1 cup packed cilantro leaves
- 2 tablespoons vegetable oil
- 2 tablespoons lime juice
- 1 teaspoon salt
- 1 teaspoon sugar
- ¼ teaspoon ground cumin

Jalapeño peppers can sting and irritate the skin; wear rubber gloves when handling peppers and do not touch eyes. Wash hands after handling.

Drop green onions, jalapeños, ginger and garlic through feed tube of food processor with motor running. Stop machine and add cilantro, oil, lime juice, salt, sugar and cumin; process until cilantro is finely chopped.

Thai-Style Pork Kabobs

⅓ cup soy sauce
2 tablespoons fresh lime juice
2 tablespoons water
2 teaspoons hot chili oil*
2 cloves garlic, minced
1 teaspoon minced fresh ginger
12 ounces well-trimmed pork tenderloin
1 red or yellow bell pepper, cut into ½-inch pieces
1 red or sweet onion, cut into ½-inch chunks

If hot chili oil is not available, combine 2 teaspoons vegetable oil and ½ teaspoon red pepper flakes in small microwavable cup. Microwave at HIGH 30 to 45 seconds. Let stand 5 minutes to allow flavor to develop.

1. Combine soy sauce, lime juice, water, chili oil, garlic and ginger in medium bowl. Reserve ⅓ cup mixture for dipping sauce.

2. Cut pork tenderloin lengthwise in half; cut crosswise into 4-inch-thick slices. Cut slices into ½-inch strips. Add to bowl with soy sauce mixture; toss to coat. Cover; refrigerate at least 30 minutes or up to 2 hours, turning once.

3. To prevent sticking, spray grid with nonstick cooking spray. Prepare grill for direct cooking.

4. Remove pork from marinade; discard marinade. Alternately weave pork strips and thread bell pepper and onion chunks onto eight 8- to 10-inch metal skewers.

5. Grill, covered, over medium-hot coals 6 to 8 minutes or until pork is barely pink in center, turning halfway through grilling time. Serve with reserved dipping sauce.

Makes 4 servings

Thai-Style Pork Kabobs

Potato Pierogi

4 medium potatoes (about 1½ pounds), peeled and quartered
⅓ cup milk
2 tablespoons butter or margarine
2 tablespoons chopped green onion
1 teaspoon salt, divided
½ teaspoon white pepper, divided
2¾ cups all-purpose flour
1 cup sour cream
1 whole egg
1 egg yolk
1 tablespoon vegetable oil
Melted butter, cooked crumbled bacon or sour cream (optional)

1. To prepare filling, place potatoes in medium saucepan; cover with water. Bring to a boil. Reduce heat and simmer, uncovered, 20 minutes or until tender. Drain; return potatoes to saucepan.

2. Mash potatoes. Stir in milk, butter, onion, ½ teaspoon salt and ¼ teaspoon pepper (mixture will be stiff). Cool.

3. To prepare pierogi dough, combine flour, sour cream, whole egg, egg yolk, oil, and remaining ½ teaspoon salt and ¼ teaspoon pepper in medium bowl; mix well.

4. Turn out dough onto lightly floured surface. Knead dough 3 to 5 minutes or until soft and pliable, but not sticky. Let rest, covered, 10 minutes. Divide dough in half. Roll out each half into 13-inch circle on lightly floured surface with lightly floured rolling pin. Cut dough into 2½-inch circles with cookie cutter.

5. Place 1 rounded teaspoon potato filling in center of each dough circle. Moisten edges of circles with water and fold in half; press edges firmly to seal.

6. Bring 4 quarts lightly salted water to a boil in Dutch oven over high heat. Cook pierogi in batches 10 minutes. Remove with slotted spoon to serving dish. Drizzle butter over pierogi, top with bacon or serve with sour cream, if desired.

Makes about 5 dozen pierogi

Potato Pierogi

Steamed Pork & Shrimp Dumplings (Siu Mai)

5 ounces tiny cooked shrimp
1 pound ground pork
½ cup finely chopped water chestnuts
2 green onions, finely chopped
1 tablespoon soy sauce
1 tablespoon dry sherry
2 teaspoons cornstarch
1 teaspoon minced fresh ginger
½ teaspoon dark sesame oil
¼ teaspoon sugar
1 egg, separated
1 tablespoon water
36 (3-inch) wonton wrappers*
36 green peas
Additional soy sauce (optional)
Chili oil (optional)

*Most markets carry square wrappers. If 3-inch round wrappers are available, omit step 3.

1. Drain shrimp on paper towels. Set aside 36 shrimp. Place remaining shrimp in large bowl. Add pork, water chestnuts, green onions, 1 tablespoon soy sauce, sherry, cornstarch, ginger, sesame oil and sugar; mix well.

2. Stir egg white into pork mixture until well blended; set aside. Place egg yolk in cup. Whisk water into egg yolk; set aside.

3. To trim square wrappers into circles, stack 12 wrappers on top of each other, keeping remaining wrappers covered with plastic wrap to prevent drying. Cut into 3-inch circles with tip of paring knife using round cookie cutter as guide. Repeat procedure 2 more times, keeping trimmed wrappers covered with plastic wrap.

4. Lightly brush each wrapper with egg yolk mixture. Spoon 1½ tablespoons pork mixture onto center of each wrapper. Bring edge of wrapper up around filling in small pleats to make basket or purse shape. Leave small opening in top to reveal a bit of filling. Set upright on clean surface pressing down slightly to flatten bottom; cover with plastic wrap. Repeat with remaining wrappers and filling.

5. To steam dumplings, place 12-inch bamboo steamer in wok. Add water to ½ inch *below* steamer. (Water should not touch steamer.) Remove steamer. Cover wok; bring water to a boil over high heat.

6. Oil bottom of bamboo steamer. Arrange half of dumplings about ½ inch apart in steamer. Brush tops lightly with egg yolk mixture; place 1 pea and 1 reserved shrimp on top of each dumpling, pressing to secure in place.

7. Place steamer in wok over boiling water; reduce heat to medium. Cover and steam dumplings about 12 minutes or until filling is firm to the touch. Remove wok from heat. Transfer dumplings to serving plate.

8. Repeat steps 6 and 7 with remaining dumplings. Serve immediately with soy sauce and chili oil for dipping, if desired. *Makes 3 dozen dumplings*

Spiced Sesame Wonton Crisps

20 (3-inch) wonton wrappers, cut in half
1 tablespoon water
2 teaspoons olive oil
½ teaspoon paprika
½ teaspoon ground cumin or chili powder
¼ teaspoon dry mustard
1 tablespoon sesame seeds

1. Preheat oven to 375°F. Coat 2 large baking sheets with nonstick cooking spray.

2. Cut each halved wonton wrapper into 2 strips; place in single layer on prepared baking sheets.

3. Combine water, oil, paprika, cumin and mustard in small bowl; mix well. Brush oil mixture evenly onto wonton strips; sprinkle evenly with sesame seeds.

4. Bake 6 to 8 minutes or until lightly browned. Remove to wire rack; cool completely. *Makes 80 crisps*

Apricot-Chicken Pot Stickers

2 cups plus 1 tablespoon water, divided
2 boneless skinless chicken breasts (about 8 ounces)
2 cups finely chopped cabbage
½ cup apricot fruit spread
2 green onions with tops, finely chopped
2 teaspoons soy sauce
½ teaspoon grated fresh ginger
⅛ teaspoon black pepper
30 (3-inch) wonton wrappers
  Sweet-and-sour sauce (optional)

1. Bring 2 cups water to a boil in medium saucepan. Add chicken. Reduce heat to low; simmer, covered, 10 minutes or until chicken is no longer pink in center. Remove from saucepan; drain.

2. Add cabbage and remaining 1 tablespoon water to saucepan. Cook over high heat 1 to 2 minutes or until water evaporates, stirring occasionally. Remove from heat; cool slightly.

3. Finely chop chicken. Add to saucepan along with preserves, green onions, soy sauce, ginger and pepper; mix well.

4. To assemble pot stickers, remove 3 wonton wrappers at a time from package. Spoon slightly rounded tablespoonful chicken mixture onto center of each wrapper; brush edges of wrapper with water. Bring 4 corners together; press to seal. Repeat with remaining wrappers and filling.

5. Spray steamer with nonstick cooking spray. Assemble steamer so that water is ½ inch below steamer basket. Fill steamer basket with pot stickers, leaving enough space between them to prevent sticking. Cover; steam 5 minutes. Transfer pot stickers to serving plate. Serve with prepared sweet-and-sour sauce, if desired.

Makes 30 pot stickers

Apricot-Chicken Pot Stickers

Lentil Patties with Coconut-Mango Relish

1¼ cups dried lentils, rinsed and sorted
Coconut-Mango Relish (recipe on facing page)
1 small onion, chopped
2 cloves garlic, minced
½ teaspoon cumin
¼ teaspoon salt
¼ teaspoon black pepper
⅛ teaspoon hot pepper sauce
1 small carrot, shredded
¼ cup all-purpose flour
1 egg
2 tablespoons chopped pitted black olives
Vegetable oil

1. Place lentils in 2-quart saucepan; cover with 2 inches water. Bring to a boil; reduce heat to low. Cover; simmer 30 to 40 minutes or until tender; drain. Spread lentils on baking sheet lined with paper towels. Let stand about 20 minutes or until lentils are cool and most of moisture has been absorbed. Meanwhile, prepare Coconut-Mango Relish; set aside.

2. Combine half of lentils, onion, garlic, cumin, salt, pepper and hot pepper sauce in food processor; process until just combined (mixture will be thick).

3. Add carrot, flour, egg and olives. Process using on/off pulsing action until well blended; transfer to large bowl. Stir in remaining half of lentils with spoon.

4. Coat bottom of large skillet with oil. Heat over medium-high heat until very hot. Shape 2 rounded tablespoonfuls of lentil mixture into patty. Repeat with remaining lentil mixture. Cook patties over medium heat 6 to 7 minutes on each side until browned on both sides, adding additional oil if needed. Serve with Relish.

Makes 4 to 6 servings

Coconut-Mango Relish

½ cup shredded unsweetened coconut
½ cup fresh cilantro
2 tablespoons chopped fresh ginger
2 tablespoons fresh lemon juice
1 tablespoon water
½ cup chopped mango

Place all ingredients except mango in food processor; process until finely chopped. Stir in mango. Cover; refrigerate up to 4 hours before serving.

Makes ½ cup relish

Shrimp Tapas in Sherry Sauce

1 slice thick-cut bacon, cut into ¼-inch strips (optional)
2 tablespoons olive oil
2 ounces crimini or button mushrooms, sliced into quarters
½ pound large shrimp (about 16 shrimp), peeled and deveined, leaving tails attached
2 cloves garlic, thinly sliced
2 tablespoons medium dry sherry
1 tablespoon lemon juice
¼ teaspoon red pepper flakes

1. Cook bacon in large skillet over medium heat until brown and crispy. Remove from skillet and drain on paper towels.

2. Add oil to bacon drippings in skillet. Add mushrooms; cook and stir 2 minutes.

3. Add shrimp and garlic; cook and stir 3 minutes or until shrimp turn pink and opaque. Stir in sherry, lemon juice and red pepper flakes.

4. Remove shrimp to serving bowl with slotted spoon. Cook sauce 1 minute or until reduced and thickened. Pour over shrimp. Sprinkle with reserved bacon.

Makes 4 servings

Chicken Satay

1 pound chicken tenders or boneless skinless chicken breasts, cut into 8 strips
2 tablespoons soy sauce

Satay Dipping Sauce
Nonstick cooking spray
2 tablespoons finely chopped onion
1 clove garlic, minced
Dash ground ginger
½ cup crunchy peanut butter
3 to 4 tablespoons soy sauce
3 to 4 tablespoons rice wine vinegar
1 teaspoon sugar

1. Place chicken in 8-inch square baking pan; drizzle with 2 tablespoons soy sauce and toss. Let stand 5 to 10 minutes.

2. Thread 1 chicken tender on metal or bamboo skewer. Repeat with remaining chicken tenders. Arrange skewers on broiler pan. Broil 4 inches from heat 3 to 5 minutes per side or until chicken is no longer pink in center.

3. Meanwhile, prepare Satay Dipping Sauce. Spray small saucepan with cooking spray; heat over medium heat. Add onion, garlic and ginger; cook and stir 2 to 3 minutes or until onion is tender. Add remaining ingredients; cook 1 minute, stirring constantly, until smooth and hot. Spoon into bowl for dipping.

4. Arrange chicken on serving platter. Serve with Satay Dipping Sauce.

Makes 8 servings

Prep and Cook Time: 30 minutes

Chicken Satay

Vietnamese Summer Rolls

Vietnamese Dipping Sauce (recipe on facing page)
8 ounces medium raw shrimp, peeled and deveined
3½ ounces thin rice noodles (rice vermicelli)
12 rice paper wrappers,* 6½ inches in diameter
36 fresh whole cilantro leaves
4 ounces roast pork or beef, sliced ⅛ inch thick
1 tablespoon chopped peanuts

*Available at specialty stores or Asian markets

1. Prepare Vietnamese Dipping Sauce; set aside.

2. Fill large saucepan ¾ full of water; bring to a boil over high heat. Add shrimp; simmer 1 to 2 minutes or until shrimp turn pink and opaque. Remove shrimp with slotted spoon to small bowl. When cool, slice shrimp in half lengthwise.

3. Meanwhile, add rice noodles to saucepan. Cook according to package directions until tender but still firm, 1 to 3 minutes. Drain in colander and rinse under cold running water to stop cooking; drain again. Cut into manageable lengths with clean scissors.

4. To form summer rolls, soften 1 rice paper wrapper in shallow bowl of warm water 30 to 40 seconds. Drain and place wrapper flat on cutting board.

5. Arrange 3 cilantro leaves upside down in center of wrapper. (These will be visible through rice paper wrapper.)

6. Layer 2 shrimp halves, flat side up, over cilantro leaves. Place layer of pork on top of shrimp. Arrange ¼ cup rice noodles over pork.

7. Fold bottom of wrapper up over filling; fold in each side. Roll up toward top of wrapper. Place on platter with cilantro/shrimp on top. Repeat with remaining wrappers and fillings.

8. Sprinkle summer rolls with peanuts. Serve with Vietnamese Dipping Sauce.

Makes 12 summer rolls

Vietnamese Dipping Sauce

½ **cup water**
¼ **cup fish sauce***
2 **tablespoons lime juice**
1 **tablespoon sugar**
1 **clove garlic, minced**
¼ **teaspoon chili oil**

Fish sauce is a Southeast Asian condiment similar to soy sauce, available in Asian markets and large supermarkets. Soy sauce may be substituted, but flavor will be different.

Combine all ingredients in small bowl; mix well.　　　*Makes about 1 cup sauce*

Caponata Spread

1½ **tablespoons BERTOLLI® Olive Oil**
1 **medium eggplant, diced (about 4 cups)**
1 **medium onion, chopped**
1½ **cups water, divided**
1 **envelope LIPTON® RECIPE SECRETS® Savory Herb with**
　 Garlic Soup Mix
2 **tablespoons chopped fresh parsley (optional)**
　 Salt and ground black pepper to taste
　 Pita chips or thinly sliced Italian or French bread

In 10-inch nonstick skillet, heat oil over medium heat and cook eggplant with onion 3 minutes. Add ½ cup water. Reduce heat to low and simmer covered 3 minutes. Stir in soup mix blended with remaining 1 cup water. Bring to a boil over high heat. Reduce heat to low and simmer uncovered, stirring occasionally, 20 minutes. Stir in parsley, salt and pepper. Serve with pita chips.　　*Makes about 4 cups spread*

Focaccia

1½ cups warm water (105 to 110°F)
1 package active dry yeast
1 teaspoon sugar
4 cups all-purpose flour, divided
7 tablespoons olive oil, divided
1 teaspoon salt
¼ cup bottled roasted red peppers, drained and cut into strips
¼ cup pitted black olives

1. Combine warm water, yeast and sugar in large bowl. Let stand 5 minutes or until bubbly. Add 3½ cups flour, 3 tablespoons oil and salt, stirring until soft dough forms. Turn out dough onto lightly floured surface. Knead 5 minutes or until smooth and elastic, gradually adding remaining flour to prevent sticking, if necessary. Shape dough into ball; place in large, lightly greased bowl. Turn dough over so top is greased. Cover with towel; let rise in warm place 1 hour or until doubled in bulk.

2. Brush 15×10-inch jelly-roll pan with 1 tablespoon oil. Punch down dough. Turn out dough onto lightly floured surface. Flatten into rectangle; roll out almost to size of pan. Place dough in pan; gently press dough to edges of pan. Poke surface of dough with end of wooden spoon handle, making indentations every 1 or 2 inches. Brush with remaining 3 tablespoons oil. Gently press peppers and olives into dough, forming decorative pattern. Cover with towel; let rise in warm place 30 minutes or until doubled in bulk.

3. Preheat oven to 450°F. Bake 12 to 15 minutes or until golden brown. Cut into squares or rectangles. Serve hot. *Makes 12 servings*

Focaccia

Dim Sum Pork Buns

1 pound frozen white bread dough
Barbecued Pork Tenderloin, chopped (recipe on facing page)
4 dried shiitake or black Chinese mushrooms
1 tablespoon peanut oil
¼ cup chopped green onions
1 tablespoon minced fresh ginger
1 tablespoon brown sugar
1 tablespoon soy sauce
1 tablespoon hoisin sauce
1½ teaspoons cornstarch
Plum Sauce (recipe on facing page)
1 egg
1 tablespoon water
1 tablespoon sesame seeds

1. Thaw bread dough and let rise according to manufacturer's directions.

2. Prepare Barbecued Pork Tenderloin.

3. To prepare filling, place mushrooms in small bowl. Cover with warm water; let stand 30 minutes. Rinse well and drain, squeezing out excess water. Cut off and discard stems. Cut caps into thin slices.

4. Heat oil in large skillet over medium heat. Add pork, mushrooms, green onions and ginger; cook and stir 2 minutes. Add sugar, soy sauce, hoisin sauce and cornstarch; cook and stir until thickened. Cool slightly.

5. Cut parchment paper or waxed paper into 16 (4-inch) squares. Place 1 inch apart on baking sheets.

6. Punch down dough. Divide dough in half; cover one half with plastic wrap. Cut remaining dough into 8 equal pieces. Shape each piece of dough into disc. Pinch edge of disc between thumb and forefinger, working disc in circular motion to form a circle 4 inches in diameter. Center should be thicker than edge.

7. Place disc flat on work surface. Place 1 heaping tablespoon filling in center. At 3 or 4 places gently lift edge of dough up around filling; pinch dough together to seal. Repeat with remaining dough and filling.

8. Place buns, seam side down, on parchment paper squares. Cover with towel; let rise in warm place 45 minutes or until doubled in bulk.

9. Prepare Plum Sauce.

10. To bake buns,* preheat oven to 375°F. Beat egg and water until well blended; gently brush onto tops of buns. Sprinkle with sesame seeds. Bake 14 to 18 minutes or until buns are golden brown and sound hollow when tapped. Serve warm with Plum Sauce.   *Makes 16 buns*

To steam buns, place 12-inch bamboo steamer in wok. Add water to ½ inch below steamer. (Water should not touch steamer.) Remove steamer. Bring water to a boil over high heat. Arrange 4 buns at a time in steamer, using parchment paper to lift. Place steamer over boiling water; reduce heat to medium. Cover and steam buns 15 minutes. To prevent splitting, turn off heat and let buns stand, covered, 5 minutes.

Barbecued Pork Tenderloin

1 tablespoon soy sauce
1 tablespoon hoisin sauce
2 teaspoons brown sugar
1 clove garlic, minced
½ teaspoon Chinese 5-spice powder
1 whole pork tenderloin (about 12 ounces)

1. Combine all ingredients except pork in large glass bowl. Add pork; turn to coat. Cover and refrigerate at least 1 hour or overnight, turning occasionally.

2. Preheat oven to 350°F. Place meat on meat rack in shallow foil-lined baking pan. Bake 30 minutes or until meat registers 155°F in center of pork. Remove meat from oven; cool slightly.   *Makes filling for 16 buns*

Plum Sauce

1 cup plum preserves
½ cup prepared chutney, chopped
2 tablespoons brown sugar
2 tablespoons lemon juice
2 teaspoons soy sauce
2 teaspoons minced fresh ginger
2 cloves garlic, minced

Combine all ingredients in small saucepan. Cook and stir over medium heat until preserves melt.   *Makes 1 cup sauce*

Tuscan White Bean Crostini

2 cans (15 ounces each) white beans (such as Great Northern or cannellini), rinsed and drained
½ large red bell pepper, finely chopped *or* ⅓ cup finely chopped roasted red bell pepper
⅓ cup finely chopped onion
⅓ cup red wine vinegar
3 tablespoons chopped fresh parsley
1 tablespoon olive oil
2 cloves garlic, minced
½ teaspoon dried oregano
¼ teaspoon black pepper
18 slices French bread, about ¼ inch thick

1. Combine beans, bell pepper and onion in large bowl.

2. Whisk together vinegar, parsley, oil, garlic, oregano and black pepper in small bowl. Pour over bean mixture; toss to coat. Cover; refrigerate 2 hours or overnight.

3. Arrange bread slices in single layer on large nonstick baking sheet or broiler pan. Broil, 6 to 8 inches from heat, 30 to 45 seconds or until bread slices are lightly toasted. Remove; cool completely.

4. Top each toasted bread slice with about 3 tablespoons bean mixture.

Makes 6 servings

Tuscan White Bean Crostini

Grilled Antipasto Platter

16 medium scallops
16 medium shrimp, shelled and deveined
12 mushrooms (about 1 inch diameter)
  3 ounces thinly sliced prosciutto or deli-style ham
16 slender asparagus spears
  1 jar (6½ ounces) marinated artichoke hearts, drained
  2 medium zucchini, cut lengthwise into slices
  1 large or 2 small red bell peppers, cut into 1-inch strips
  1 head radicchio, cut lengthwise into quarters (optional)
  Lemon Baste (recipe follows)

Soak 12 long bamboo skewers in water for at least 20 minutes to keep them from burning. Thread 4 scallops on each of 4 skewers and 4 shrimp on each of another 4 skewers. Thread 6 mushrooms on each of 2 more skewers. Cut prosciutto into 2×1-inch strips. Wrap 2 asparagus spears together with 2 strips of prosciutto; secure with a toothpick. Repeat with remaining asparagus spears. Wrap each artichoke heart in 1 strip of prosciutto; thread on 2 remaining skewers. Place ingredients except radicchio and lemon wedges on a baking sheet. Reserve ¼ cup Lemon Baste. Brush remaining Lemon Baste liberally over ingredients on baking sheet.

Spread medium KINGSFORD® Briquets in a wide single layer over the bed of the grill. Oil hot grid to help prevent sticking. Grill skewers, asparagus bundles, zucchini and red peppers, on an uncovered grill, 7 to 12 minutes until vegetables are tender, seafood firms up and turns opaque and prosciutto around wrapped vegetables is crisp, turning once or twice. Remove each item from grill to a large serving platter as it is done. Pour remaining baste over all. Serve hot or at room temperature. Garnish with radicchio and lemon wedges.

Makes 8 appetizer servings or 4 main-dish servings

Lemon Baste

  ½ cup olive oil
  ¼ cup lemon juice
  ½ teaspoon salt
  ¼ teaspoon black pepper

Whisk together all ingredients in small bowl until well blended.

Makes about ¾ cup

Asian Vegetable Rolls with Soy-Lime Dipping Sauce

¼ **cup soy sauce**
 2 **tablespoons lime juice**
 1 **teaspoon honey**
 1 **clove garlic, crushed**
½ **teaspoon finely chopped fresh ginger**
¼ **teaspoon dark sesame oil**
⅛ **to** ¼ **teaspoon red pepper flakes**
½ **cup grated cucumber**
⅓ **cup grated carrot**
¼ **cup thinly sliced yellow bell pepper, cut into 1-inch strips**
 2 **tablespoons thinly sliced green onion**
18 **small leaf lettuce leaves or Bibb lettuce leaves from inner part of head**
   Sesame seeds (optional)

1. Combine soy sauce, lime juice, honey, garlic, ginger, oil and red pepper flakes in small bowl.

2. Combine cucumber, carrot, bell pepper and green onion in medium bowl.

3. Add 1 tablespoon soy sauce mixture to vegetable mixture; stir to combine. Place about 1 tablespoon vegetable mixture on each lettuce leaf. Roll up leaves and top with sesame seeds at time of serving, if desired. Serve with remaining sauce.

Makes 6 servings

Prep Time: 15 minutes

Party Time

Pepper Cheese Cocktail Puffs

½ package (17¼ ounces) frozen puff pastry, thawed
1 tablespoon Dijon mustard
½ cup (2 ounces) finely shredded Cheddar cheese
1 teaspoon cracked black pepper
1 egg
1 tablespoon water

1. Preheat oven to 400°F. Grease baking sheets.

2. Roll out 1 sheet puff pastry dough on well floured surface to 14×10-inch rectangle. Spread mustard over half of dough from 10-inch side. Sprinkle with cheese and pepper. Fold dough over filling; roll gently to seal edges.

3. Cut lengthwise into 3 strips; cut each strip diagonally into 1½-inch pieces. Place on prepared baking sheets. Beat egg and water in small bowl; brush onto appetizers.

4. Bake appetizers 12 to 15 minutes or until puffed and deep golden brown. Remove from baking sheet to wire rack; cool.   *Makes about 20 appetizers*

Tip: Work quickly and efficiently when using puff pastry. The colder puff pastry is, the better it will puff in the hot oven. This recipe can be easily doubled.

Prep and Bake Time: 30 minutes

Pepper Cheese Cocktail Puffs

Mariachi Chicken

1 ¼ cups crushed tortilla chips
1 package (1 ounce) LAWRY'S® Taco Spices & Seasonings
2 dozen chicken drummettes or 1 pound boneless chicken breasts
Salsa and sour cream (optional)

In large resealable plastic bag, combine chips and Taco Spices & Seasonings. Dampen chicken with water; shake off excess. Place a few pieces at a time in bag; seal and shake to coat with chips. Arrange in greased shallow baking pan. Bake, uncovered, in preheated 350°F oven for 40 to 45 minutes, until chicken is thoroughly cooked. Serve with salsa and sour cream, if desired.

Makes 24 appetizers or 4 main dish servings

Meal Idea: Serve with Mexican rice and/or refried beans and a crisp green salad or coleslaw.

Prep Time: 5 to 10 minutes
Cook Time: 40 to 45 minutes

Hotsy Totsy Spiced Nuts

1 can (12 ounces) unsalted mixed nuts
3 tablespoons *Frank's® RedHot®* Original Cayenne Pepper Sauce
1 tablespoon vegetable oil
¾ teaspoon seasoned salt
¾ teaspoon garlic powder

1. Preheat oven to 250°F. Place nuts in 15×10-inch jelly-roll pan. Combine remaining ingredients in small bowl; pour over nuts. Toss to coat evenly.

2. Bake 45 minutes or until nuts are toasted and dry, stirring every 15 minutes. Cool completely.

Makes about 2 cups mix

Prep Time: 5 minutes
Cook Time: 45 minutes

Mariachi Chicken

Smoked Salmon Lavash

4 ounces cream cheese, softened
1 tablespoon lemon juice
¼ teaspoon prepared horseradish
4 small (about 5 inches) lavash* flat breads
4 ounces sliced smoked salmon
½ red onion, thinly sliced
2 tablespoons capers, drained

*Lavash (also spelled lahvosh) is a thin, crisp Middle-Eastern flat bread. Other flat breads or toasts may be substituted.

Combine cream cheese, lemon juice and horseradish in small bowl. Spread carefully over lavash. Top with salmon, onion and capers.   *Makes 4 servings*

Zesty Liver Pâté

⅓ cup butter or margarine
1 pound chicken livers
¾ cup coarsely chopped green onions
¾ cup chopped fresh parsley
½ cup dry white wine
¾ teaspoon TABASCO® brand Pepper Sauce
½ teaspoon salt
Crackers or French bread

Melt butter in large saucepan; add chicken livers, onions and parsley. Sauté until livers are evenly browned and cooked through. Transfer to blender or food processor container. Add wine, TABASCO® Sauce and salt; cover. Process until smooth. Pour into decorative crock-style jar with lid. Chill until thick enough to spread. Serve with crackers or French bread.   *Makes about 2 cups pâté*

Smoked Salmon Lavash

Party Stuffed Pinwheels

1 envelope LIPTON® RECIPE SECRETS® Savory Herb with Garlic Soup Mix*
1 package (8 ounces) cream cheese, softened
1 cup shredded mozzarella cheese (about 4 ounces)
2 tablespoons milk
1 tablespoon grated Parmesan cheese
2 packages (10 ounces each) refrigerated pizza crust

Also terrific with LIPTON® RECIPE SECRETS® Onion Soup Mix.

1. Preheat oven to 425°F. In medium bowl, combine all ingredients except pizza crusts; set aside.

2. Unroll pizza crusts, then top evenly with filling. Roll, starting at longest side, jelly-roll style. Cut into 32 rounds.**

3. On baking sheet sprayed with nonstick cooking spray, arrange rounds cut side down.

4. Bake, uncovered, 13 minutes or until golden brown.   *Makes 32 pinwheels*

**If rolled pizza crust is too soft to cut, refrigerate or freeze until firm.*

Lipton® Ranch Dip

1 envelope LIPTON® RECIPE SECRETS® Ranch Soup Mix
1 container (16 ounces) sour cream

1. In medium bowl, combine ingredients; chill, if desired.

2. Serve with your favorite dippers.   *Makes 2 cups dip*

Ranch Salsa Dip: Stir in ½ cup of your favorite salsa.

Ranch Artichoke Dip: Stir in 1 jar (14 ounces) marinated artichoke hearts, drained and chopped.

Prep Time: 5 minutes

Party Stuffed Pinwheels

Party Cheese Spread

1 cup ricotta cheese
6 ounces cream cheese, softened
1 medium onion, chopped
2 tablespoons grated Parmesan cheese
1 tablespoon drained capers
2 anchovy fillets, mashed *or* 2 teaspoons anchovy paste
1 teaspoon dry mustard
1 teaspoon paprika
½ teaspoon hot pepper sauce
   Red cabbage or bell pepper

1. Beat ricotta cheese and cream cheese in large bowl with electric mixer on medium speed until well blended. Stir in onion, Parmesan cheese, capers, anchovies, mustard, paprika and hot pepper sauce; mix well. Cover; refrigerate at least 1 day or up to 1 week to allow flavors to blend.

2. Just before serving, remove and discard any damaged outer leaves from cabbage. Slice small piece from bottom so cabbage will sit flat. Cut out and remove inside portion of cabbage, leaving a 1-inch-thick shell. (Be careful not to cut through bottom of cabbage.) Spoon cheese spread into hollowed-out cabbage. Serve with crackers and raw vegetables. Garnish if desired.   *Makes about 2 cups spread*

Party Cheese Spread

Fiesta Chicken Nachos

1 tablespoon olive oil
1 pound boneless, skinless chicken breasts
1 jar (1 pound) RAGÚ® Cheesy! Double Cheddar Sauce
1 bag (9 ounces) tortilla chips
2 green and/or red bell peppers, diced
1 small onion, chopped
1 large tomato, diced

In 12-inch skillet, heat olive oil over medium-high heat and cook chicken, turning occasionally, 8 minutes or until thoroughly cooked. Remove from skillet; cut into strips.

In same skillet, combine chicken and Ragú Cheesy! Double Cheddar Sauce; heat through.

On serving platter, arrange layer of tortilla chips, then ½ of the sauce mixture, bell peppers, onion and tomato; repeat, ending with tomato. Garnish, if desired, with chopped fresh cilantro and shredded lettuce.   *Makes 4 servings*

Recipe Tip: For a spicier dish, add chopped jalapeño peppers or hot pepper sauce.

Lipton® Onion Dip

1 envelope LIPTON® RECIPE SECRETS® Onion Soup Mix
1 container (16 ounces) sour cream

1. In medium bowl, combine ingredients; chill, if desired.

2. Serve with your favorite dippers.   *Makes 2 cups dip*

Salsa Onion Dip: Stir in ½ cup of your favorite salsa.

Prep Time: 5 minutes

Fiesta Chicken Nachos

Texas-Style Stuffed Pizza Bread

1 package (13.8 ounces) refrigerated pizza crust
⅓ cup *French's*® *Gourmayo*™ Smoked Chipotle Light Mayonnaise
½ pound sliced deli roast beef
¼ pound sliced mozzarella or Jack cheese
1 jar (7½ ounces) roasted red peppers, drained and sliced
1 cup sautéed onions*
1 teaspoon olive oil
1 teaspoon crushed oregano leaves
1 teaspoon minced garlic

*Tip: To sauté onions, cook 1½ cups sliced onions in 1 tablespoon oil for 5 minutes or until tender.

1. Heat oven to 425°F. Roll pizza dough into 13×10-inch rectangle on floured work surface. Spread mayonnaise evenly on dough. Layer roast beef and cheese on dough, overlapping slices, leaving a 1-inch border around edges. Top with peppers and onion.

2. Fold one-third of dough toward center from long edge of rectangle. Fold second side toward center enclosing filling. Tightly pinch long edge and ends to seal. Place seam-side down on greased baking sheet.

3. Brush with oil; sprinkle with oregano and garlic. Cut shallow slits crosswise along top of dough, spacing 3 inches apart. Bake 18 to 20 minutes or until deep golden brown. Remove to rack; cool slightly. Serve warm.   *Makes 12 servings*

Prep Time: 20 minutes
Cook Time: 20 minutes

Texas-Style Stuffed Pizza Bread

Seafood Crêpes

Basic Crêpes (recipe on facing page)
3 tablespoons butter
⅓ cup finely chopped shallots or sweet onion
2 tablespoons dry vermouth
3 tablespoons all-purpose flour
1½ cups plus 2 tablespoons milk, divided
¼ to ½ teaspoon hot pepper sauce (optional)
8 ounces cooked peeled and deveined shrimp, coarsely chopped (1½ cups)
8 ounces lump crabmeat or imitation crabmeat (1½ cups)
2 tablespoons snipped fresh chives or green onion tops
3 tablespoons freshly grated Parmesan cheese
Fresh chives and red onion for garnish

1. Prepare Basic Crêpes. Preheat oven to 350°F.

2. Melt butter over medium heat in medium saucepan. Add shallots; cook and stir 5 minutes or until shallots are tender. Add vermouth; cook 1 minute.

3. Add flour; cook and stir 1 minute. Gradually stir in 1½ cups milk and hot pepper sauce, if desired. Bring to a boil, stirring frequently. Reduce heat to low; cook and stir 1 minute or until mixture thickens.

4. Remove from heat; stir in shrimp and crabmeat. Reserve ½ cup seafood mixture.

5. To assemble crêpes, spoon about ¼ cup seafood mixture down center of each crêpe. Roll up crêpes jelly-roll style. Place seam side down in well-greased 13×9-inch baking dish.

6. Stir chives and remaining 2 tablespoons milk into reserved seafood mixture. Spoon seafood mixture down center of crêpes; sprinkle cheese evenly over top.

7. Bake uncovered 15 to 20 minutes or until heated through. Serve immediately.

Makes 12 crêpes

Basic Crêpes

1½ cups milk
1 cup all-purpose flour
2 eggs
¼ cup (½ stick) butter, melted, cooled and divided
¼ teaspoon salt

1. Combine milk, flour, eggs, 2 tablespoons butter and salt in food processor; process using on/off pulsing action until smooth. Let batter rest covered in refrigerator 1 hour or no more than 30 minutes at room temperature.

2. Heat ½ teaspoon butter in 7- or 8-inch crêpe pan or skillet over medium heat. Pour ¼ cup batter into hot pan. Immediately rotate pan back and forth to swirl batter over entire surface of pan.

3. Cook 1 to 2 minutes or until crêpe is brown around edges and top is dry. Carefully turn crêpe with spatula and cook 30 seconds more. Repeat with remaining batter, adding remaining butter only as needed to prevent sticking.

4. Stack cooled crêpes. Wrap airtight; refrigerate up to 1 day or freeze up to 1 month. Thaw before filling and serving. *Makes about 1 dozen crêpes*

tip

Crêpes are excellent party food since they can be made in advance and freeze beautifully. To thaw crêpes quickly, wrap them in foil and place in a 250°F oven for about 30 minutes until warmed through. Crêpes can be wrapped around all sorts of fillings both savory and sweet. For a simple but delicious treat, spread crêpes with a good quality jam and cream cheese and roll or fold.

Stuffed Party Baguette

2 medium red bell peppers
1 loaf French bread (about 14 inches long)
¼ cup plus 2 tablespoons Italian dressing, divided
1 small red onion, very thinly sliced
8 large fresh basil leaves
3 ounces Swiss cheese, very thinly sliced

1. Preheat oven to 425°F. Cover large baking sheet with foil; set aside.

2. To roast bell peppers, cut peppers in half; remove stems, seeds and membranes. Place peppers, cut sides down, on prepared baking sheet. Bake 20 to 25 minutes or until skins are blackened.

3. Transfer peppers from baking sheet to paper bag; close bag tightly. Let stand 10 minutes or until peppers are cool enough to handle and skins are loosened. Peel off and discard skins. Cut peppers into strips.

4. Trim ends from bread; discard. Cut loaf lengthwise in half. Remove soft insides of loaf; reserve removed bread for another use, if desired.

5. Brush ¼ cup Italian dressing evenly onto cut sides of bread. Arrange pepper strips in even layer in bottom half of loaf; top with even layer of onion. Brush onion with remaining 2 tablespoons Italian dressing; top with layer of basil and cheese. Replace bread top. Wrap loaf tightly in heavy-duty plastic wrap; refrigerate at least 2 hours or overnight.

6. When ready to serve, remove plastic wrap. Cut loaf crosswise into 1-inch slices. Secure with toothpicks. *Makes 12 servings*

Stuffed Party Baguette

Peppery Brie en Croûte

2 (4-ounce) packages crescent roll dough
1 (8-ounce) wheel Brie cheese
2 tablespoons TABASCO® brand Green Pepper Sauce
1 egg, beaten
Crackers

Preheat oven to 375°F. Work crescent roll dough into thin circle large enough to completely wrap cheese. Place cheese in center of dough circle. Prick top of cheese several times with fork. Slowly pour 1 tablespoon TABASCO® Green Pepper Sauce over top of cheese. Let stand briefly for sauce to sink in.

Add remaining 1 tablespoon TABASCO® Green Pepper Sauce, pricking cheese several more times with fork. (Some sauce will run over side of cheese.) Bring edges of dough over top of cheese, working it together to completely cover cheese. Brush edges with beaten egg and seal. Bake about 10 minutes, following directions on crescent roll package. (Do not overbake, as cheese will run.) Serve immediately with crackers. *Makes 8 to 10 servings*

Fruit Antipasto Platter

2 cups fresh DOLE® Tropical Gold® Pineapple, cut into wedges
2 medium, firm DOLE® Bananas, sliced diagonally
2 oranges, peeled and sliced
½ cup thinly sliced DOLE® Red Onion
½ pound low fat sharp Cheddar cheese, cut into 1-inch cubes
2 jars (6 ounces each) marinated artichoke hearts, drained and halved
DOLE® Green or Red Leaf Lettuce
½ cup fat free or light Italian salad dressing

• Arrange fruit, onion, cheese and artichoke hearts on lettuce-lined platter; serve with dressing. Garnish, if desired. *Makes 10 servings*

Peppery Brie en Croûte

Toasted Pesto Rounds

¼ cup thinly sliced fresh basil or chopped fresh dill
¼ cup grated Parmesan cheese
3 tablespoons mayonnaise
1 medium clove garlic, minced
12 French bread slices, about ¼ inch thick
1 tablespoon plus 1 teaspoon chopped fresh tomato
1 green onion with top, sliced
Black pepper

1. Preheat broiler.

2. Combine basil, cheese, mayonnaise and garlic in small bowl; mix well.

3. Arrange bread slices in single layer on large ungreased nonstick baking sheet or broiler pan. Broil 6 to 8 inches from heat 30 to 45 seconds or until bread slices are lightly toasted.

4. Turn bread slices over; spread evenly with basil mixture. Broil 1 minute or until lightly browned. Top evenly with tomato and green onion. Season to taste with pepper. Transfer to serving plate. *Makes 12 appetizers*

Reuben Bites

24 party rye bread slices
½ cup prepared Thousand Island dressing
6 ounces turkey pastrami, very thinly sliced
1 cup (4 ounces) shredded Swiss cheese
1 cup alfalfa sprouts

1. Preheat oven to 400°F.

2. Arrange bread slices on nonstick baking sheet. Bake 5 minutes or until lightly toasted.

3. Spread 1 teaspoon dressing onto each bread slice; top with pastrami, folding slices to fit bread slices. Sprinkle evenly with cheese.

4. Bake 5 minutes or until hot. Top evenly with sprouts. Transfer to serving plate
Makes 24 pieces

Toasted Pesto Rounds

Cheddar Cheese and Rice Roll

2 cups cooked UNCLE BEN'S® ORIGINAL CONVERTED® Brand Rice
3 cups grated low-fat Cheddar cheese
¾ cup fat-free cream cheese, softened
1 can (4½ ounces) green chilies, drained, chopped
⅛ teaspoon hot sauce
1½ cups chopped walnuts

PREP: CLEAN: Wash hands. Combine rice, Cheddar cheese, cream cheese, chilies and hot sauce. Mix by hand or in food processor. Shape mixture into a log. Roll in walnuts. Wrap tightly with plastic wrap and refrigerate 1 hour.

SERVE: Serve with assorted crackers.

CHILL: Refrigerate leftovers immediately. *Makes 15 servings*

PREP TIME: 20 minutes

Easy Cheese Fondue

1 pound low-sodium Swiss cheese (Gruyère, Emmentaler or
combination of both), shredded or cubed
2 tablespoons cornstarch
1 garlic clove, crushed
1 cup HOLLAND HOUSE® White or White with Lemon Cooking Wine
1 tablespoon kirsch or cherry brandy (optional)
Pinch nutmeg
Ground black pepper

1. In medium bowl, coat cheese with cornstarch; set aside. Rub inside of ceramic fondue pot or heavy saucepan with garlic; discard garlic. Bring wine to gentle simmer over medium heat. Gradually stir in cheese to ensure smooth fondue. Once smooth, stir in brandy, if desired. Garnish with nutmeg and pepper.

2. Serve with bite-sized chunks of French bread, broccoli, cauliflower, tart apples or pears. Spear with fondue forks or wooden skewers. *Makes 1¼ cups*

Cheddar Cheese and Rice Roll

Easy Spinach Appetizer

2 tablespoons butter
3 eggs
1 cup milk
1 cup all-purpose flour
1 teaspoon baking powder
1 teaspoon salt
2 packages (10 ounces each) frozen chopped spinach, thawed and well drained
4 cups (16 ounces) shredded Monterey Jack cheese
½ cup diced red bell pepper

1. Preheat oven to 350°F. Melt butter in 13×9-inch pan.

2. Beat eggs in medium bowl. Add milk, flour, baking powder and salt; beat until well blended. Stir in spinach, cheese and bell pepper; mix well. Spread mixture over melted butter in pan.

3. Bake 40 to 45 minutes or until set. Let stand 10 minutes before cutting into triangles or squares. *Makes 2 to 4 dozen pieces*

tip

Easy Spinach Appetizer can also be made ahead, frozen and reheated. After baking, cool completely and cut into squares. Transfer squares to cookie sheet; place cookie sheet in freezer until squares are frozen solid. Transfer to resealable food storage bag. To serve, reheat squares in preheated 325°F oven for 15 minutes.

Easy Spinach Appetizer

Brandy-Soaked Scallops

1 pound bacon, cut in half crosswise
2 pounds small sea scallops
½ cup brandy
⅓ cup olive oil
2 tablespoons chopped fresh parsley
1 clove garlic, minced
1 teaspoon black pepper
½ teaspoon salt
½ teaspoon onion powder
Salad greens (optional)

1. Wrap one piece bacon around each scallop; secure with toothpick, if necessary. Place wrapped scallops in 13×9-inch baking dish.

2. Combine brandy, oil, parsley, garlic, pepper, salt and onion powder in small bowl; mix well. Pour mixture over scallops; cover and marinate in refrigerator at least 4 hours.

3. Remove scallops from marinade; discard marinade. Arrange scallops on rack of broiler pan. Broil 4 inches from heat 7 to 10 minutes or until bacon is brown. Turn over; broil 5 minutes more or until scallops are opaque. Remove toothpicks. Arrange over salad greens and garnish, if desired. *Makes 8 servings*

tip

The scallop is a bivalve with beautiful fan-shaped shells. It is usually sold already shucked. Purchase your scallops from a reputable market and look for those with a fresh smell and a creamy or pinkish beige color. Be suspicious of stark white scallops as they were probably soaked in a solution to prolong their freshness. These scallops will have a compromised flavor and texture and will be difficult to brown because of the excess water they have absorbed. Frozen scallops are a better bet.

Brandy-Soaked Scallops

Chicken Parmesan Stromboli

1 pound boneless, skinless chicken breast halves
½ teaspoon salt
¼ teaspoon ground black pepper
2 teaspoons olive oil
2 cups shredded mozzarella cheese (about 8 ounces)
1 jar (1 pound 10 ounces) RAGÚ® Chunky Pasta Sauce, divided
2 tablespoons grated Parmesan cheese
1 tablespoon finely chopped fresh parsley
1 pound fresh or thawed frozen bread dough

1. Preheat oven to 400°F. Season chicken with salt and pepper. In 12-inch skillet, heat olive oil over medium-high heat and brown chicken. Remove chicken from skillet and let cool; pull into large shreds.

2. In medium bowl, combine chicken, mozzarella cheese, ½ cup Ragú Chunky Pasta Sauce, Parmesan cheese and parsley; set aside.

3. On greased jelly-roll pan, press dough to form 12×10-inch rectangle. Arrange chicken mixture down center of dough. Cover filling bringing one long side into center, then overlap with the other long side; pinch seam to seal. Fold in ends and pinch to seal. Arrange on pan, seam-side down. Gently press in sides to form 12×4-inch loaf. Bake 35 minutes or until dough is cooked and golden. Cut stromboli into slices. Heat remaining pasta sauce and serve with stromboli. *Makes 6 servings*

Chicken Parmesan Stromboli

Tiny Vegetable Boats

1 can (15½ ounces) chick-peas, drained and rinsed
1 large clove garlic, peeled
¼ cup fresh lemon juice
2 ounces chicken broth
¼ teaspoon white pepper
¼ teaspoon dried thyme
16 white mushrooms
¼ cup sliced pimiento
16 medium grape or cherry tomatoes
16 fresh snow peas

1. In food processor fitted with chopping blade, process chick-peas, garlic, lemon juice, broth, white pepper and thyme. Process until mixture is smooth, stopping to scrape down side of work bowl with rubber spatula. Transfer mixture to small bowl; cover and refrigerate.

2. Wash, dry and stem mushrooms. Scoop out caps slightly with small melon ball scoop or tip of vegetable peeler. Using teaspoon, fill each mushroom cap with chick-pea mixture, mounding slightly. Place mushrooms on serving plate. Garnish each with 1 pimiento strip cut to fit. Cover loosely with plastic wrap; refrigerate until ready to serve.

3. Halve tomatoes lengthwise. Using tip of vegetable peeler, scrape out seeds, juice and membranes; drain cut sides down on paper towels. Using teaspoon, fill tomato halves with chick-pea mixture, mounding slightly. Place on serving plate. Cover loosely with plastic wrap; refrigerate until ready to serve.

4. Wash, dry and trim snow pea pods. Spread remaining chick-pea mixture on curved side of each snow pea. Place on serving plate. Cover loosely with plastic wrap; refrigerate until ready to serve. *Makes 48 appetizers*

Hearty Nachos

1 pound ground beef
1 envelope LIPTON® RECIPE SECRETS® Onion Soup Mix
1 can (19 ounces) black beans, rinsed and drained
1 cup prepared salsa
1 package (8½ ounces) plain tortilla chips
1 cup shredded Cheddar cheese (about 4 ounces)

1. In 12-inch nonstick skillet, brown ground beef over medium-high heat; drain.

2. Stir in soup mix, black beans and salsa. Bring to a boil over high heat. Reduce heat to low and simmer 5 minutes or until heated through.

3. Arrange tortilla chips on serving platter. Spread beef mixture over chips; sprinkle with Cheddar cheese. Top, if desired, with sliced green onions, sliced pitted ripe olives, chopped tomato and chopped cilantro.   *Makes 8 servings*

Prep Time: 10 minutes
Cook Time: 12 minutes

Eggplant Caviar

1 large eggplant, unpeeled
¼ cup chopped onion
2 tablespoons lemon juice
1 tablespoon olive or vegetable oil
1 small clove garlic
½ teaspoon salt
½ teaspoon TABASCO® brand Pepper Sauce
    Sieved hard-cooked egg white (optional)
    Lemon slices (optional)

Preheat oven to 350°F. Place eggplant in shallow baking dish. Bake 1 hour or until soft, turning once. Trim off ends; slice eggplant in half lengthwise. Place cut-side-down in colander and let drain 10 minutes. Scoop out pulp; reserve pulp and peel. Combine eggplant peel, onion, lemon juice, oil, garlic, salt and TABASCO® Sauce in blender or food processor. Cover and process until peel is finely chopped. Add eggplant pulp. Cover and process just until chopped. Place in serving dish. Garnish with egg white and lemon slices, if desired. Serve with toast points.   *Makes 1½ cups*

Acknowledgments

The publisher would like to thank the companies and organizations listed below for the use of their recipes and photographs in this publication.

American Lamb Council

Bob Evans®

Dole Food Company, Inc.

Florida Department of Agriculture and Consumer Services, Bureau of Seafood and Aquaculture

The Hershey Company

The Hidden Valley® Food Products Company

Hillshire Farm®

Holland House® is a registered trademark of Mott's, LLP

Hormel Foods, LLC

The Kingsford® Products Co.

Lawry's® Foods

MASTERFOODS USA

McIlhenny Company (TABASCO® brand Pepper Sauce)

Minnesota Cultivated Wild Rice Council

National Fisheries Institute

National Pork Board

Ortega®, A Division of B&G Foods, Inc.

Reckitt Benckiser Inc.

Sargento® Foods Inc.

Sonoma® Dried Tomatoes

Southeast United Dairy Industry Association, Inc.

StarKist Seafood Company

The Sugar Association, Inc.

Unilever Foods North America

Wisconsin Milk Marketing Board

Index

METRIC CONVERSION CHART

VOLUME MEASUREMENTS (dry)

1/8 teaspoon = 0.5 mL
1/4 teaspoon = 1 mL
1/2 teaspoon = 2 mL
3/4 teaspoon = 4 mL
1 teaspoon = 5 mL
1 tablespoon = 15 mL
2 tablespoons = 30 mL
1/4 cup = 60 mL
1/3 cup = 75 mL
1/2 cup = 125 mL
2/3 cup = 150 mL
3/4 cup = 175 mL
1 cup = 250 mL
2 cups = 1 pint = 500 mL
3 cups = 750 mL
4 cups = 1 quart = 1 L

VOLUME MEASUREMENTS (fluid)

1 fluid ounce (2 tablespoons) = 30 mL
4 fluid ounces (1/2 cup) = 125 mL
8 fluid ounces (1 cup) = 250 mL
12 fluid ounces (1 1/2 cups) = 375 mL
16 fluid ounces (2 cups) = 500 mL

WEIGHTS (mass)

1/2 ounce = 15 g
1 ounce = 30 g
3 ounces = 90 g
4 ounces = 120 g
8 ounces = 225 g
10 ounces = 285 g
12 ounces = 360 g
16 ounces = 1 pound = 450 g

DIMENSIONS

1/16 inch = 2 mm
1/8 inch = 3 mm
1/4 inch = 6 mm
1/2 inch = 1.5 cm
3/4 inch = 2 cm
1 inch = 2.5 cm

OVEN TEMPERATURES

250°F = 120°C
275°F = 140°C
300°F = 150°C
325°F = 160°C
350°F = 180°C
375°F = 190°C
400°F = 200°C
425°F = 220°C
450°F = 230°C

BAKING PAN SIZES

Utensil	Size in Inches/Quarts	Metric Volume	Size in Centimeters
Baking or Cake Pan (square or rectangular)	8×8×2	2 L	20×20×5
	9×9×2	2.5 L	23×23×5
	12×8×2	3 L	30×20×5
	13×9×2	3.5 L	33×23×5
Loaf Pan	8×4×3	1.5 L	20×10×7
	9×5×3	2 L	23×13×7
Round Layer Cake Pan	8×1½	1.2 L	20×4
	9×1½	1.5 L	23×4
Pie Plate	8×1¼	750 mL	20×3
	9×1¼	1 L	23×3
Baking Dish or Casserole	1 quart	1 L	—
	1½ quart	1.5 L	—
	2 quart	2 L	—